I DON'T LIVE THERE ANYMORE

Doug Oldham

with Fred Bauer

I DON'T LIVE THERE ANYMORE

impact books

Nashville, Tennessee

ACKNOWLEDGEMENTS

Our thanks to the following publishers for permission to quote from the following copyrighted materials.

GAITHER MUSIC
   Thanks To Calvary
      © copyright 1969 by William J. Gaither;

   He Touched Me
      © copyright 1963 by William J. Gaither.

SINGSPIRATION, INC.
   Let Me Lose Myself And Find It Lord In Thee
   Renewal 1971. Assigned to Singspiration, Inc.

   Follow Me
      © copyright 1953 by Singspiration, Inc.

   I Know Who Holds Tomorrow
      ©copyright 1950 by Singspiration, Inc.

TYNDALE HOUSE.
   ©Copyright   1971 by Tyndale House Publishers
   Psalm 32. The Living Bible.

Library of Congress Catalog Card Number: 73-75986.

DEDICATION

Dedicated to Laura Lee whose love and forgiveness have been surpassed only by His

And not many days after the younger son gathered all together, and took his journey into a far country . . .

And when he had spent all, there arose a mighty famine in that land; and he began to be in want. . . .

And when he came to himself, he said . . .

"I will arise and go to my father, and will say unto him, 'Father, I have sinned against heaven and before thee. . . .' "

And he arose, and came to his father. . . .

And the son said unto him, "Father, I have sinned against heaven, and in thy sight, and am no more worthy to be called thy son."

But the father said to his servants, "Bring forth the best robe, and put it on him; and put a ring on his hand, and shoes on his feet:

And bring hither the fatted calf, and kill it; and let us eat, and be merry:

For this my son was dead, and is alive again; he was lost, and is found." And they began to be merry.

Luke 15:13-24

INTRODUCTION:
Why This Book Was Written
by Fred Bauer

The spotlight carves a small circle of light out of the blinding darkness . . . within the confines of the light stands a chunk of a man, singing . . . he is unconfined . . . his movements are relaxed and easy . . . his round face freely changing from one expression to another, and his voice . . . powerful, full of pathos and deep conviction . . . glides effortlessly over the notes like a boy skipping stones across a farm pond . . . behind him, somewhere in the night, an orchestra of fifty violins, violas, cellos, basses, horns, trumpets, trombones, flutes, clarinets, oboes and drums . . . rides with the growing excitement this man's singing creates . . . so does the choir which races to catch his inspiring crescendo . . . the crowd of several thousands is mutually linked by the electricity that fills the air . . . they don't move, don't cough or seemingly breathe as the song's finish comes closer . . . it is a gospel ballad about a lost, defeated, hopeless man who has miraculously found his way out of misery into a victorious life of faith . . . the man singing doesn't tell the audience that the song is about his own life . . . but, instinctively, they know.

Doug Oldham has this kind of charisma when he sings. I wasn't sure that I believed it when others first told me about him; I thought they must surely be exaggerating. They weren't.

He is all that they have said and more. After I heard him, saw people respond to his message and witnessed lives changed as a direct result of his musical ministry, I came to understand. Well, not really. Understanding Doug Oldham may be something like trying to understand the theory of relativity. He marches to his own drumbeat. He resists regimentation, cliches, pigeon-holing, easy answers. All of which may be why it took him so long to get his life squared away. It also may help explain why—once he found the path—he has climbed at such a rapid pace. But I'm getting ahead of myself. I want to tell you how I came to know Doug, and how I got involved in this project. It is illustrative, I think, of the rapport that this man builds between people.

I was overcommitted on several writing projects when Bob Benson came to New York and approached me about helping Doug write his life story. It was November of 1971 and the John T. Benson Publishing Company wanted the work begun immediately. Though I had heard the name Doug Oldham, I wasn't sure I was the one to do the book and I doubted that I could find the time.

Bob Benson isn't a guy who's easily discouraged, however. A week after our meeting, I received some background information about the singer as well as several of his albums. "Listen to these," Bob wrote. "He is a rare and gifted singer." I read the material and looked over the liner copy on the albums. A comment by Harry Bristow, president of the National Evangelical Film Foundation, caught my eye: "Doug Oldham communicates a faith . . . a faith to help you climb the mountains of life. It seems as if God has sent this special voice for times such as these." With that ringing endorsement, I had every intention of listening to the albums that very night, but something kept me from it. Weeks went by before I thought of them. Meanwhile, Bob came to see me again. This time we had lunch and once more he talked to me about working on the book. He told me of Doug's dramatic story—how his life had hit rock bottom, how his spiritual comeback had been an inspiration to so many others and how his singing ministry was growing.

I remember well the story Bob related about Ronn Huff, arranger and conductor for some of Doug's latest records. The two had met several years before when Doug was still leading a dual life, and Ronn apparently had sensed something phoney about him. They had not hit it off very well, and this social distance remained even after their paths crossed again. Then, one day in a London recording studio, Ronn heard Doug sing Bill Gaither's great song "Thanks to Calvary." Ronn was sitting outside the recording booth as a spectator waiting to conduct on the following session. When Doug finished, he came out of the booth shaking his head. "I'm sorry, I'll do it again." While he was singing a very meaningful phrase, his voice had broken with emotion and he thought he had ruined the "take."

"Oh, no, you don't," said the producer, Bob MacKenzie, with tears in his eyes. "That one should go into the album as it is." Later, Ronn commented that it was at that point that he knew Doug Oldham was for real. Here was a man who believed implicitly in the words he sang. In those moments, a rich friendship was to begin.

After my second meeting with Bob, I still didn't agree to take the assignment, but was intrigued enough to go home that night and listen to the albums. After dinner, I moved into the living room, put another log on the fire (it was snowing outside), turned on the record player and sat back to listen to this much touted singer. What I heard was an unusual, sensitive, deeply moving voice—a voice that was full of belief and conviction. Doug Oldham wasn't just singing words, he was pouring out his heart and soul. He was sharing himself.

Before the last album was on the turntable, I went to the phone and called Bob in Nashville. "When can I meet Doug Oldham?" I asked.

A week later, the two of us got together in a Midwestern

city where Doug had come to sing. We talked from 11:00 a.m. until nearly six o'clock when he had to leave for the church. He told me straightforwardly, warts and all, about the life he had led in his "rotten B.C. (before Christ) days" and how the Lord had pulled him out of that hole and had blessed him since. Several times, as he recalled painful experiences, he wiped away tears. The same honest sincerity I had heard on the album was there as he talked to me. It was a part of his fabric.

"Before I leave," I said, "there's one last question I want to ask you: Why do you want to do the book?"

"Because I believe the Good News is still good," he said, smiling.

Three weeks later, we began work on the story you now hold in your hands. While researching it, I came to know the Doug Oldham that others had been telling me about. And I came to know the Doug only he himself knew as he told me about himself. It was a traumatic experience for Doug to recount some of the incidents of his life, but they help prove that the Good News *is* still good. I was able to see how God has blessed Doug Oldham when I traveled to his home in Alexandria, Indiana, not far from where I grew up in Ohio. It is the same kind of small Midwestern town as the one in which I lived as a kid—a Main Street lined with businesses for a couple of blocks, two-storey houses with porch swings and big yards, a deserted railroad station, a basket and backboard on almost every garage, a volunteer fire department, free-running dogs and plenty of kids.

There in Alexandria, in the Oldhams' century-old, antique-laden brick house, we worked for several days. It was fun getting acquainted with all the Oldhams; Doug, his talented wife, Laura Lee, and their three bright, confident, refreshingly open teen-age daughters. Theirs is not a stodgy faith, but a practical, positive, happy one. I also visited with Bill Gaither and observed the respect and mutual admiration which the two men hold for each other. Since college days, they have been friends and have worked and sung together. I made some notes of some of the things Bill had to say about Doug: "He was the first one to take my numbers and give them light," he confided. "After I wrote 'He Touched Me,' I showed it to Doug first. He took the song, sang it, recorded it and, more than anyone else, was responsible for bringing attention to it. Dozens of others have recorded it since, but no one has given quite the same sensitive interpretation of it that Doug has. Of course, I've come to expect something unique from everything Doug does. People puzzle over his communicative genius, but I don't. I think it is simply that he is an inspired singer who believes what he sings. God blesses and empowers that kind of singing."

After several days in Alexandria, it came time for a trip and we headed for Detroit in Doug's converted Greyhound bus. Though it is comfortable and can provide seats and sleeping facilities for several people, its primary purpose is to transport the elaborate sound equipment Doug uses. I asked him if so much equipment was necessary and he answered, "Quality is as important in church music as in any other kind."

That night I saw how much it added as an audience of two thousand filled a high school auditorium which normally seats about twelve hundred. People were in the aisles, on the floor and on the stage. Others were turned away. I'd heard about singers taking audiences in the palms of their hands, but seldom have I seen it so tangibly demonstrated. When the invitation was given at the close of the evening, scores responded.

Afterward, we were whisked to Metropolitan Airport where a twin-engine Cessna was standing by to take Doug, his pianist, David Redman, and me to Lynchburg, Virginia. By early 1971, Doug's demanding schedule required him to travel well over 200,000 miles annually and be away from home more than 275 nights a year. In the fall Doug had become soloist on

The Old Time Gospel Hour. Now, each Saturday night—from points all over the compass—Doug climbs aboard a private plane (dispatched by the Thomas Road Baptist Church) and wings toward Lynchburg. There, each Sunday, he sings in the morning service which is televised nationwide on over four hundred stations to an audience estimated at thirty million people.

On the flight to Lynchburg that night—we would arrive in time for Doug to get only four hours' sleep before the telecast—I asked him if all the travel didn't sometimes get to him. "The toughest part of my life is being away from home, but I'm grateful for the opportunity. It gives me another way to tell people that the Good News is still good."

Grateful. I'd heard him use that same word over and over in our taping sessions. Whatever else Doug Oldham is, he is grateful. He is grateful for God's grace, grateful for parents who stood by him through the desperate years, grateful to a wife and children who forgave him, grateful for an area of service where he can speak to people about the most important thing in his life—his faith.

That gratitude was very evident as I sat in the Thomas Road Baptist Church the following morning and listened along with nearly four thousand others who filled the sanctuary for the service. There were eight thousand in Sunday School that morning. In just fifteen years this new church, under the pastorate of personable Jerry Falwell, has attracted twelve thousand members. No wonder it has been hailed as the fastest-growing church in America.

The response to Doug's singing on television is the same as it is in person or on record—positive. And people who hear him are often moved to action, to follow his counsel and to reorder their lives.

Jerry Falwell, who preaches each Sunday on the Old Time Gospel Hour, told me, "Doug's my kind of singer. He can do dozens of things with one short song: bless, soothe, convict, testify, invite, entertain, love, inspire, encourage. No singer I know can comfort the afflicted or afflict the comfortable like Doug."

As soon as the service was over, we returned to the airport and flew off for another service that night eight hundred miles away. By the time we reached the church, unfed, it was 6:30, an hour away from the evening service. Doug's bus was outside; inside, Charley Silvey, who doubles as sound technician and bus driver, had the speakers in place and ready for testing. Doug sang for a few minutes and Dave Redman played the grand piano nearby. Both were satisfied. Half an hour later, the service began. Three thousand people showed up. They were not disappointed. Afterward, Doug stayed to talk with the many who wanted to tell him what his singing had meant to them. It was nearly eleven o'clock before he had chatted with the last one.

Hungry and tired, we found a restaurant at 11:15. It was well past midnight when we reached the motel. Early the next morning, we were again on our way—this time to California for a series of rallies. Two days later, I begged off and flew back to New York, leaving Doug with three more nights of singing before he would make it home for a couple of days' rest. Then, it would be back on the road again.

On the jet East, as I thumbed through my voluminous notes, I asked myself this question: "Why would anyone go through such a physically draining ordeal night after night, week after week, month after month?" No sooner had the thought passed through my mind than I found the answer in some of my earliest jottings, ones I'd made when I was still uncertain that I would take the assignment. It was all wrapped up in the reply Doug had given me when I asked him why he wanted to write a book.

"To tell people that the Good News is still good."

That's why this story—Doug's story—was written.

TABLE OF CONTENTS

PROLOGUE
Thanks To Calvary

It all seems so simple to me now. It just seems impossible that it was so close all along and that it took me so long to find the way. It's funny to think that I finally came right back to what I had run from for so many years.

One night recently I was singing in a concert in a city in the Midwest. The concert was held in a lovely civic auditorium that was filled to overflowing with a sellout crowd of 4,500 people. I had on a specially-made, extra-large tuxedo. When you are my size, you don't buy many clothes off the racks. Someone said it looked like a slipcover for a haystack!

The concert was a singer's delight, for accompanying me was a huge orchestra made up of the city's finest symphony players. There was also a choir, and the arrangements were designed to provide a thrilling backdrop of orchestral and vocal sound. It was a big night for me, also, because I had been traveling for over three weeks and Laura and the girls had flown in for the evening. When I finished, the audience rose to its feet and I stood there, drenched in the warmth of the spotlight and the love and friendship of the ringing applause.

It had been a wonderful evening for me. At intermission, a young woman had come hesitantly backstage and asked a member of the stage crew if she could see me for a moment.

He brought her over to where I was sitting, and we talked until the flashing lights reminded us that it was time for her to return to her seat and for me to pause for a moment of quiet before singing again.

"I want you to know that you kept me from losing my mind," she said. "About two years ago, I was backing our car out of the garage and ran over our little girl. I held her in my arms as the ambulance rushed her to the hospital, but there was nothing that could be done for her. When we finally left the hospital, I asked my husband to take me to a motel for the rest of the night. I just couldn't face home and that driveway."

"In the room, I tried to read and to go to sleep, but my mind was shattered with grief and guilt. I could only pace the floor. My husband wanted me to take a sedative, but I refused. I switched on the TV and you were on the channel, singing 'Take Your Burden to the Lord and Leave it There.' I hadn't heard that old song since I was a child, for I'd drifted away from God and the church. I slipped down on my knees and asked for His forgiveness and for His help in bearing the burden of the nightmare through which I was living. Before you had finished singing, He had begun to do all that I had asked and more. I don't know where I'd be today, Doug, if you hadn't been singing that song—that night—for me."

"No, not thanks to me—thanks to *Calvary*."

After the houselights had come back on and the audience was moving toward the exits, a well-dressed couple approached me, and I sat down on the edge of the stage to talk with them. They had the easy, relaxed look that affluence brings. They told me they had been in town for a national sales convention and had stayed over for the concert.

"We have all the things that are supposed to make people happy—the house, the cars, children, friends, security, but something has always been missing from our lives. When you sang 'Thanks to Calvary,' we suddenly knew what was wrong. Right there in our seats, we asked Him to fill the emptiness. Now, we too can say, 'Thanks to Calvary, we don't live there anymore.' "

As I walked out into the night, my mind was filled with people—people who had come to me in person or written me a letter saying, "Thanks to Calvary, I'm not what I used to be."

I thought of the fine-looking boy in his late teens who had come to me after a service on the West Coast to say, "Thanks to Calvary, I'm off drugs." The words of the song had convinced him that he could get off the hook—that he didn't have to go back anymore.

And there was the woman a few weeks ago in North Carolina who came to me with her face aglow to tell me about her daughter: "Alice has been in a mental institution for nearly two years. Next week, she's coming home!"

"Wonderful," I began. But the mother had more to tell.

"Doctors had held little hope of her ever getting well. Then, one day, I took her one of your albums which included many of my favorites. One of them was 'Thanks to Calvary.' Alice played it several times a day. After two weeks, her psychiatrist called me aside, 'I don't know what's happening, but something has changed. Alice is a different girl,' he told me. Four weeks later, they told me she was going to be well. Last week her doctor said she could come home. Thanks to Calvary!"

I thought of the letters that have come in from all over—from hospitals, jails, prisons, military bases. Most of them are notes of praise to God. Of course, some of the stories are like unfinished symphonies—but at least they are in tune with the Master Conductor.

I thought of the night in Michigan when I was heading back to my motel on foot. A car pulled alongside, and the driver yelled, "Hey, Doug, want a lift?"

"Sure," I told the man, a stranger to me.

I got in, and in the few seconds it took to reach my room, he told me all about himself. He watched the "Old Time Gospel Hour" every Sunday. "Wouldn't miss it." He told me he was a beer salesman.

"But I'm thinking of changing jobs."

"Oh," I answered, noncommittally.

"Don't you think I should?"

"What's the Lord telling you to do?"

"To find a new job."

"Then, that's your answer. In fact, I wouldn't be surprised to find that He already has one picked out for you."

And I thought about a recent night in New Jersey when I was singing in a large church which must have seated twenty-five hundred comfortably. Nearly three thousand had jammed every available space for this Saturday night concert. There were people in the aisles, on the platform, around the piano and almost under my feet. When I came out to begin the service, it seemed the audience had to inhale to give me a place to stand. Of course, I require a little more space than the "average bear."

In spite of the conditions, it was an exciting service. I sang for more than an hour the songs that mean the most to me and many requests—songs such as "Something Good is Going to Happen to You," "He Touched Me," "A Rich Man Am I," "Something Worth Living For," "Happiness," "Family of God," "If It Keeps Gettin' Better," "The King is Coming," and many others. I also gave my testimony, telling how God had lifted me from a life of sin and aimlessness. When we finished, the altar call was given and a lot of people came forward—many of them young people, teen-agers like my own three girls.

After the service, when nearly everyone had gone and I was ready to leave, a man was waiting for me at the back door of the church.

"Doug," he said, "have you got a minute?"

"Sure," I told him, and I followed him over to a corner where he began talking confidentially. I learned quickly that he was a brand-new Christian and that, after a life of drinking and running around with other women, he was trying to make the crooked places straight.

"Before you sang 'Thanks to Calvary' tonight, you said that God helped you deal with a broken home. My wife and I are separated, but I want my family back. She can't believe that I've turned over a new leaf, and she won't give me another chance."

He pushed his dark, wavy hair back from his forehead and looked at the floor, feeling all the weight of his thirty-five years. "I doubt if you have any idea how much of a rat I've been," he said, "and how badly I've hurt my wife."

"Yes, I know," I nodded. "I've been down that road, and if you'll drive me to the airport, I'll tell you about it."

As we crossed town, I told him that I knew all too well the things he was talking about and how I'd been able to build a new life on the foundation of God's love and forgiveness. I told him I knew God would do the same for him.

"Do you really think so?" he said, with tears in his eyes.

"I know so," I replied.

Before I climbed out of his car and into the plane, we prayed together. "Lord Jesus," I prayed, "help John, here, to know that You love him and want the best for him. Help him to reach his wife, melt her resistance and fill her with understanding. Bring them back together again. Give them faith to trust each other and to make their marriage a good one again."

Then John prayed, asking for the words to say to his wife.

When I left, I told him not to give up, to keep praying and to believe that God would work things out for the best. A few weeks later, I received a letter from John. He and his wife and children were back together again. The family had dedicated themselves and their home to Christ.

John wrote that he had just about given up, believing that a broken home was the price God was going to exact from him for his promiscuous ways. "But when I heard your story, I decided to call my wife once more. This time she listened . . . thanks to Calvary!"

Walking down the street behind the girls—Karen and Dee-Dee and Paula—my arm about Laura, my heart was overflowing with joy and bubbling with thanks . . . "thanks to Calvary."

It hasn't always been this way. Most of my life has been spent within a stone's throw of the church. With the exception of a very short period of time, the songs I have sung have been religious songs. I was raised in a parsonage, went to church colleges and earned most of my livelihood as a minister of music. But, always, I was searching—running from job to job, city to city, church to church, friend to friend—trying to shake the agony of guilt and shame that dogged my footsteps everywhere I went. When I think of the abject failure and the new beginnings that made up my life before I let Christ in completely, I can hardly realize how I could have failed to see the way for so long. Like the prodigal son, I found it isn't far to the "far country."

If you were ever as lonely and guilty as I was and had come to something like this—you'd know—you'd know why I sing with every fiber of my being "thanks to Calvary, I don't live there anymore." This is my story—the story behind my song.

Doug Oldham

CHAPTER 1
Face The Music

As usual, I was late for my appointment. I wheeled the little green Ford into the parking lot alongside the church. It was midafternoon on a hot, muggy day, and I choked when the dust cloud my car had stirred up caught me as I opened the door. The handle burned my hands as I pushed it shut and started across to the side door of the church in the blazing afternoon sun.

I entered the building and started down the steps to his office. It became progressively cooler with each step I took. Each step also increased the gnawing fear that this meeting was going to be like dozens of others in the past—with my parents, with teachers, with deans, with other pastors where I had served as a minister of music.

I paused for a moment before knocking on his study door. I listened to him inside talking on the phone—thankful for a few more seconds before I faced the failure and guilt that I had come to know so well.

I doubt that the meeting was any easier for him. He was my pastor and my boss, because I was serving his church as minister of music. But he was also my friend. My dad had been kind of a spiritual father to him, and he had known me through my family for a long time. It was his friendship that had brought us to his town and his church when I needed a place to go after my last series of failures.

A couple of hours earlier, he had called and asked me to meet him in his study. There was a bit of sadness and urgency in his voice that told me this was not a meeting to plan for Sunday's music or to "drop in on the Greens" as he jokingly said when we took an afternoon off to play golf together.

When he called I wasn't dressed or shaved, for I had slept most of the morning hours away, as usual. Laura just let me sleep, postponing the inevitable grumbling and complaining she would have to hear.

I knocked gently, opened the door, entered his office and moved across the room. He nodded toward a chair, and I sat down and waited as he finished his telephone conversation.

When he had hung up the receiver, we sat for a moment. The only sound in the room came from the air conditioner as it labored under the double burden of hot weather and old age.

Finally, he broke the silence, "Doug, there are rumors going about the church that you are having an affair. This is a small church, and what one person knows is soon known by everybody. Before you say anything, I think you should know that one of the board members says that he saw you coming out of a hotel in a nearby city with a woman. He named the hotel, the town and the woman."

"Doug," he continued, "you've got to tell me if this is true."

His voice seemed to indicate that he was afraid it was so, yet was desperately hoping that it wasn't. His tone and his manner suggested that even if it were, he was still my friend and in some way would stand by me.

I had deceived myself and others so long that it was easy for me to deny the whole thing. Because he had named the wrong town and the wrong time, I replied firmly, "That is not true."

"I'm glad," he said. "However, because of the seriousness

of the rumor, I think the board will want you to meet with them and answer any questions they might have."

In my mind I was already packing. I was renting the trailer and getting the boxes from the grocery store. I had run before and I would run again. It was the same song, but a different verse. It had happened to me before, and it would happen again before I finally found a stopping place. It could have been any one of a dozen places or situations, for I had played this tune so many times before, I could do it from memory. It seemed that the pattern of my life was set—sin, guilt, deception, discovery and running. I didn't know much about staying but I knew all about running. It was like trying to pack both your present failures and your future hopes in the same set of boxes. It was trying to fool yourself that it was the people around you who were the problem, when all the time, you knew it was you. Loading up, pulling out, moving in, starting over, but it all added up to running.

"I'll be happy to see the board and clear my name," I said as I left, but I knew that I couldn't and wouldn't see them.

On the way home I relived it all in my mind. I remembered the mild flirtation and the cautious acceptance. I remembered the day the teasing turned to seriousness and I remembered with shame the cheapness and fear that had filled me that afternoon. I remembered driving blocks out of my way from then on just to keep from going by the hotel.

But I wasn't ready yet to admit the truth to anyone.

"Laura, we're leaving this place," I stormed indignantly when I returned home. "Somebody in this church is out to get me, and they have started a rumor that I have been having an affair. Now, they want me to meet the board and answer questions. If they don't have any more confidence in me and in what I have done here, we'll just leave."

By the following Sunday, I had found a new position and had made my plans to leave . . . to run again . . . from God and myself.

CHAPTER 2

Heritage And Childhood Days

Later that night, pacing the floor, I looked back—way back. Laura was asleep, the light from the living room silhouetting her sleeping form. Contemplating her rising and falling profile should have filled me with some feelings of warmth and pride, I suppose. After all, my first child was riding in her womb. But, as usual, my thoughts were turned to myself and my problems. I was somewhat aware of what I was doing to Laura. In turning to others for companionship, conversation, understanding, I was rejecting her. It only increased my own frustration and defeat to realize I was causing her great worry and anguish. I was tortured by spiritual guilt combined with a fear of being discovered, of knowing that I was not what I wanted people to think I was. Yet, somehow, I continued to hurt her. I felt that I loved her, but my actions contradicted the statement completely.

Flopping down in my favorite chair in the living room, I snapped off the lights and sat in the near-darkness. Only the flickering blue-yellow flame from the gas log pierced the blackness. I wanted to shut out all that had happened to me—if I could just wish it away. But the darkness seemed only to invite all the old miseries, all the failures and guilt, and they rolled endlessly over me during that long night.

Where did it all begin? How could I have gotten myself

into such a fix? If I had come from a broken and Godless home, if my parents had been unloving and uncaring, if there had been some terrible, tragic event to blame . . . if only I could have found something or someone to accuse except myself. I had nothing to point to—only a box of fragmentary clues—a drawerful of childhood mementos—a rabbit's foot on a chain, a Valentine from a third-grade sweetheart, a blue ribbon from a spelling bee, a bone-handled knife with a broken blade, a picture of myself on a scooter, a seashell from our vacation to the East Coast, a cat's eye marble, a faded high school pennant—puzzle pieces which didn't fit or add up to any shape or design. Where was the answer?

My father was a pastor like his father before him. For two generations, the lives of the Oldhams had revolved around the church. Dad was born in the Oklahoma territory, but shortly afterward, his family moved to Iowa where he spent his boyhood days. Life on the prairie must have been rugged, because he still illustrates his messages with stories of hardships and trials from his childhood memories.

When Dad was sixteen, he left home to go to the Anderson Bible Training School in Anderson, Indiana. Traveling as a young song evangelist during his school years led him to Huntington, Indiana where he met and fell in love with Pauline Edith Brown (Polly), a local girl who played the piano for the meeting. After their marriage and brief honeymoon, they continued as traveling evangelists. Later, they settled in Cynthiana, Kentucky and pastored a little flock of people who met for services in a second-floor room over the fire department. The salary was $9.00 a week, and the rent was $20.00 a month. It was here that they had their first child. If the child was a boy, they planned to name him Dean. It was a boy, stillborn, but they gave him the name and laid him and a part of their sorrowing hearts to rest in a tiny, unmarked grave.

After another interlude of evangelistic traveling, my parents accepted a church in Akron, Indiana, where their second son was born. They named him Douglas Reed.

When I was three months old, we moved to Lima, Ohio. About my only memories there are of the little red, brick schoolhouse that had been converted into our home. When I was three years old, my parents felt called to accept the pastorate of the West Third Street Church of God in Dayton, Ohio. It was to be home for me until I was in high school.

The depression had been hard on the church, and when Dad met the board for the first time, there were some pressing financial needs. Somewhat to the surprise of the men on the board, he insisted that the church begin to tithe its income for missions. Some felt that the immediate bills should be paid first, and what was left over could be sent to help others. But Dad explained the Lord would help those who put Him first, and the board adopted the plan. Some of the members borrowed money from the banks in their own names to pay off some of the church bills. From that moment on, the work began to grow and prosper. Dad hadn't been at the church long when he secured time on radio station WSMK for fifteen-minute broadcasts at 6:15 each morning. Polly played as they sang together, and Dad brought the short message. Later, he moved to WING and conducted a one-half hour Sunday afternoon broadcast. He had a fine radio voice, and he was also hired by the station to do the 6:00 a.m. and the 10:00 p.m. newscasts. An effective pastor, he was to become one of the most respected ministers in the Church of God.

Our first home in Dayton was a duplex which was quite a distance from the church. My first real buddy, Gordie Eaton, lived across the street. I remember my parents taking us to the zoo in Cincinnati. Dad continued to look for a place closer to the church, and we moved into a bungalow at 4240 Midway Avenue. It was a great place for a growing boy. Out back, a ravine and a creek separated us from a wooded area that covered two or three blocks. I loved to play in the creek and in those woods. In the spring and summer, we built endless dams in the creek. One afternoon, when that ceased to be fun, Dick Stump and I went next door and threw stones at the fish in Mrs. Clippinger's goldfish pond. Polly spotted me out the window and told my Dad. Instead of giving me a spanking when he came home, he made me go over and help clean out the pool. Later, Polly made me apologize to Mrs. Clippinger.

Maybe I ought to tell you how I started calling my mother Polly. When I was very small, I called her "Munner." Then, one afternoon, she asked me to pick up the blocks in my room. Not too enthusiastic about the whole thing, I was moving very slowly. When she rushed me, I said, "Give me time, Polly." It tickled her, and for some reason I just kept calling her "Polly." I even tried to call my Dad, Dale, once. Maybe I should say twice, for it was both the first and last time!

I remember I liked the winters and could hardly wait for it to snow. Dad used to attach a box on our sled and pull me to the store. He would wrap me in blankets until I could just barely see out. The neighborhood kids used to spend the evenings sledding on a great hill just outside our front door. The hilltop was illuminated by a streetlight, and it swooped down into complete darkness. The backyard also made a great sled-run in the daytime. You had to maneuver between a couple of thorn trees on the way down and duck at the right time to miss some limbs covered with thorns. Once, I ducked too soon and ran headlong into the tree, giving the sled and the tree a good banging up—not to mention myself.

Although I had friends that I played with, I spent a great deal of time by myself. Polly was protective—I suppose she sensed that I would be her only living child. She didn't like for me to play in the woods behind the house. They ran up into Third Street across from the Veterans' Hospital. I think she was afraid there might be some poor, demented man in the woods. Once, I caught pneumonia which nearly proved fatal. Polly wrapped me in cotton vests soaked with camphor until I was well. Sometimes, it seemed I was always wrapped up. She was afraid I would get hurt or dirty or something—and I usually did.

As a result, I played by myself a lot, and out of my loneliness, I invented friends and playmates. The most real companion was Teddy, who was an older brother to me. He was with me for several years and was so real in my mind that people often remarked to my parents that they didn't realize there were two children in the family.

Teddy and I used to play elevator by laying a card table on its side and bending the leg up and down to operate the door. Teddy would let me run the elevator, but he had a motorcycle that I was never allowed to ride. He represented a Jack Armstrong who could do everything I wished I could have done.

When I was about seven, my folks borrowed $1,000.00 from Art and Marie Piper, friends and members of the church, and bought a two-storey, white frame house across the street at 4307 Midway. Later, they used the equity to build a brick house about a block away at 360 Roxbury Road. When we moved into the new house, Roxbury was a cobblestone street. I remember how excited I was the day they came to pave it with asphalt, making it perfect for skating. The new house was across the street from City Park. Although we had lived in three houses, they were all in the same neighborhood. I knew all the things that little boys always know—the creeks, shortcuts, sled-runs, dogs, vacant lots and hiding places. I also knew every step of the eight blocks to the grammar school.

I never did really like school. I know it will be hard for you to believe, but all through elementary school, I was about normal weight, anemic and weak. I always liked recess, except that I was always the last kid chosen on the ballteam, and

I never was much good at king-on-the-hill. This was partly because of my innate lack of ability and partly because Polly insisted that I not get my school clothes dirty.

In the fourth grade, I fell in love with my teacher whose name was Miss Herwitz. She smelled like a flower garden, and I was much older before I realized that much of her appeal came from House of Stuart mouthwash and colognes.

Westwood Junior High School was about a mile away from my house. I either walked or rode the Residence Park streetcar and transferred to the Westwood bus to get to school, reversing the route in the afternoon. Pulling the trolley arm down from the wire above on the streetcar was considered great sport among the crowd that rode to school.

While at Westwood, I was thrilled to be selected to sing in a civic choir. The Inland Container Corporation had a large plant in Dayton, and one of their public relations' projects was the Inland Children's Chorus, composed of twelve to fifteen-year-olds. It was quite an honor to be chosen because of the Christmas concerts with the Dayton Symphony, held each year in Memorial Hall. Ben Westbrock was the conductor. The year before I was chosen, the group had traveled to Europe, stopping in Washington to sing for the President. Of the 140 kids who practiced, only one hundred performed, so I was pleased to be selected as a regular. The girls were dressed in frilly formals, and the boys wore Eaton collars and cutaway coats. Memorial Hall was packed for the two Christmas concerts. I had sung in church before, but this was the most exciting thing I had ever done.

My father was a conscientious and busy pastor. While he was at Dayton, the congregation doubled in size. His faithfulness to the job kept him away from home a lot of the time that I would have liked to have been with him. Occasionally, I went calling with him, but I spent most of my time with Polly.

She often read Bible stories to me and admonished me to

follow the examples of David and Jonathan and Joseph. She would play the piano in the afternoons and I would sing. Polly was very proud of my singing ability, and when I was only four, I sang at a national convention before an audience of six thousand people.

Being a good pianist herself, Polly was determined that I would learn to play, too. Like many kids, I resisted. I was about six when Marie Marks, my piano teacher, strolled up our walk for the first time. She led me into the den off the living room to the little mahogany-finished, upright piano and introduced me to the scale. She got fifty cents an hour, and though that was the going rate, she was grossly underpaid, for it was a long sixty minutes for both of us. The only period of time that was longer for me was the hour when I was required to practice by myself. Polly would call me in from play and march me to the piano. I played until she left the room. Then, I'd quit. "Douglas," she would call from the kitchen or maybe the basement, "are you practicing?" Then, I'd start another exercise before drifting off again. Most of the time I spent staring out the window, feeling sorry for myself.

After six years of negligible progress on the piano, Polly, Dad, Marie Marks and I gave up. It was clear that I would never be a child prodigy. Later, I studied briefly under Ada Clyde Gallagher at the Dayton Conservatory. I always liked her name. It had a nice sound—like Edgar Allen Poe. Though I paid for the lessons myself out of the money I earned at Kroger's, I was really taking lessons to please my parents. When I quit the piano this time, it was for good. How dumb can you get?

My family spent some of our summers at the Northern Indiana Campgrounds at Yellow Lake. Dad would come over for a few days—as often as he could get away from his duties at the church and the radio broadcast. It was about a three-hour drive, and I always looked forward to his arrival.

Since Dad was a good swimmer, he taught me how to float and then to swim during those summers at Yellow Lake. We had a small fishing boat with a Bendix air-cooled motor. The motor was huge because of the air cooler, but it was actually only about two horsepower. It would barely push the boat along. Because of the size of the motor, someone was always wanting to race, and I would have to make some excuse about not feeling like racing this morning, or something.

Our cottage was on the side of a hill with the kitchen on the backside on stilts. The folks named it the Dalene Retreat. Overlooking the lake, it was a restful spot for my parents. One of the summers Polly was sick and the Dalene Retreat made a good place for convalescing.

On holidays and during the camps in August, people came out to the grounds in droves. During the rest of the summer, there were very few people around. It was so dull that when Mr. Powell, the caretaker, got out the mower, it was a big day.

On Thursdays, Mrs. Powell baked and sold homemade bread. We bought two loaves each week, but the real treat was to bring it home still warm and cover a slice with butter and brown sugar.

Like Dad, Polly was a tireless worker in the church. She was a model preacher's wife. When someone in the church died, she would take over the household for the family until after the funeral. If someone was sick, she was the first one there to fix the meals and iron the clothes. Both of my parents were people who excelled and dedicated their talents to building the church. They strived for perfection, and they believed that if they prodded, prayed and persevered, I would do the same. My solution was to pretend to be the perfect little boy they wanted me to be. It was only a small deception at first.

The family life and, thus, mine revolved around the life of the church. Church attendance for us, of course, meant Sunday mornings, Sunday nights, Wednesday nights and all the special meetings in between. It seemed to me we were always at church. In church, Dad expected his son to be a model of piety and reverence.

Once, when I was about eleven, I was sitting with the Halley kids up near the front of the church, and we got to cutting up. Suddenly, Dad quit preaching. Everything became un-healthily quiet.

"Douglas," he thundered in a voice that sounded as if it were coming from on high, "go sit with your mother. We'll talk about this when we get home." Red-faced, I got to my feet and made the long walk to the other side of the church, all eyes watching. He did not continue until I was seated beside Mother. For some reason, I didn't get a spanking or a lecture when we got home. He must have figured the church episode was punishment enough, and it was.

On another occasion, the Halley kids got me into trouble again. On Promotion Day, just before we went upstairs, the Halleys were looking intently into a tube like a kaleidoscope. When I asked them to let me see, they said I was too young, and besides, I was the preacher's kid. Finally, I talked them into it and held the tube close to my eye. When I handed it back, there was a black, greasy circle on my face. I tried, in vain, to wash it off. Even though it was Promotion Sunday, I was too scared and embarrassed to go upstairs, so I stayed in the basement while my friends got their diplomas.

There were some fine people in the church, and some of them were especially kind to me. One was an old, humpbacked man with thin, gray hair whose name was Pfifer. He and I were conspirators. He always wore a sweater-vest under his suit coat, and he would sneak licorice drops out of the vest and slip them to me in church. I really didn't like licorice, but I always took them and traded them later for peppermint drops.

Then, there was Paul Yoder—Brother Yoder to the church people. He was a small, active man with deep-set, dancing eyes. He was teacher of the junior boys' class, and we were a boisterous crew. One Sunday, we were so bad that Brother Yoder decided not to come back the next Sunday—to the classroom, that is. He packed a picnic lunch and took us all to the creek. He had us kick off our shoes, stick our bare feet in the water, and then he filled our hands and mouths with sandwiches. This done, he calmly proceeded to tell us Bible stories.

When I was ten, I sang "The Holy City" in church one Sunday morning. To my utter dismay, the song just literally went to pieces. Somehow, the heavenly city didn't quite descend on us that day. Bill Peak, one of my friends in the church, came to me afterward and slipped me an 1882 silver dollar. I still have it.

Art and Marie Piper, members of the church, didn't have any children of their own, so they kind of adopted me. How I loved them. They were always bringing me gifts—the kind that Polly and Dad could not or would not have considered buying. For example, one Christmas, they gave me a huge racetrack with sleek racing cars. It was a knockout. I was so excited I got sick.

But the biggest event in the church year, as far as I was concerned, was the annual trip to the Church of God Camp Meeting in Anderson in June. It came right on the heels of school and, sometimes, I managed to be excused from the last couple of classes to go early with Polly and Dad. Once, it lasted for ten days—from Friday through the second Sunday. Today, the meetings are from Tuesday through Sunday.

How I anticipated that trip to Anderson every June! And what a spectacle it was driving into the campgrounds. It was like going to the circus. A huge frame structure formed a hub in the center of the grounds. In days gone by, hundreds of tents would be pitched around it by families attending the convention. Now, travel trailers are more common than tents. After arriving and getting settled, the adults would saunter off to meet with long-time friends, some of whom they saw only once a year at the convention. If we could pull it off, we kids would bug out of the meetings and run off to play. It was a fascinating place with many enticing things to explore. Penned in by the old Anderson-to-Muncie interurban on one side, by Fifth Street on another, the college on a third and, finally, a farm, we had the run of the place. I was free to roam anywhere I wanted on the grounds. I guess the folks thought kids couldn't get into much trouble in the company of the saints.

So many pleasant memories come to mind—the adventure of sleeping outdoors (one of the rules was never to touch the top of the tent when it rained), going down to the farm and helping the old guy fill campers' ticks with straw, visiting the bookstore, swimming at the local pool, playing tag, following blind Oscar Wild, the Pied Piper with accordion from one end of the camp to the other . . .

But as I began to get a little older, it seemed that the denomination and the local congregation were very strict. In the eyes of the church, anything that had any fun connected with it was wrong. Naturally, my parents were concerned that I live up to the church's codes and standards.

Every Saturday, the kids in the neighborhood, Dick and Ronnie Stump and Dick Grice, went to Skateland. I was not allowed to go roller-skating. Of course, movies were taboo also, and I was often called a sissy because I couldn't go anywhere or do anything.

Although my parents acted as if I could make my own decisions, issues were usually presented in such a way as to leave me little choice. They would say, "Now, we aren't going to say you can't go, but of course, you know there will be people there who are not Christians, and they will be doing unChristian things, and it will embarrass us if you are there, and some of the church members will criticize us for letting you go, but you can 'make your own decision.' "

If it was some borderline case where there was no strong guideline about right and wrong, their argument was always that it might be a "stumbling block" for others. This was always the "clincher."

Sometimes, though, the "rules" were almost funny. When I was fourteen, I was asked to be lifeguard during the youth camp at Yellow Lake—since I could swim and we had the boat. The church did not believe in mixed bathing, so the boys swam at one time and the girls at another. When it was the girls' turn, I had to anchor out in the lake and face away from the swimmers. If someone was about to drown, the counselor would yell to me and I was to hoist the anchor and row as rapidly as possible to save the drowning lass!

Being the preacher's son in the midst of a church with such strong convictions about every part of one's life was doubly hard for me. While there were some people in the church who lavished praise and attention on me, there were others who felt it was their responsibility to help raise the preacher's kid, and they were constantly hammering at me:

"Doug, you especially should know better."

"I think your father should be told about this."

"Doug, just because you're the minister's son . . ."

At the time, I really didn't agree with much the church dictated, but now I am glad that I was raised in a church that said *something* about what it meant to live for Christ. Today, I find myself going back to the very principles I either laughed at or rebelled against when I was growing up.

These scattered incidents are the memories that come to mind and, though I was deeply rebellious at the time, I find they are guideposts for me now. I believe in the verse that says: "Train up a child in the way he should go: and when he is old, he will not depart from it." These are the insights on which I rely now as Laura and I bring up our girls.

There was one thing I did like about the church at the time

for sure—and that was the girls. By the time I was twelve, I had begun to pick up weight, and it became obvious to me that I wasn't cut out to be a "fighter." If I was to be anything, it would have to be a "lover."

The first time I fell in "love," it was with a schoolmate named Suzanne who was the most beautiful girl I had ever seen. Unfortunately, she was totally oblivious of me, and I could never bring myself to tell her my true feelings about her. Finally, I saved enough lunch money to buy her a small, blue bottle of Evening in Paris perfume for Christmas. The mother of one of my buddies wrapped it for me, because I didn't want Polly to know. On the fateful day I took the gift to school, I carried it in a brown paper bag until school was over, trying to muster up the courage to give it to Suzanne. Finally, I caught up with her about a block from her house. She was with a couple of other girls, but I managed to blurt out: "Here's a Christmas present for you, Suzie."

I think the depth of my feeling was matched only by the height of her surprise. She wouldn't accept the gift, and I was left standing on the corner as she and her friends giggled down the street. I went home and bawled.

But I recovered and began to devote more and more of my time to the fairer sex. While the other guys my age were playing ball, I was walking the girls home from school. The boys thought I was a real fruitcake anyway because I was not very athletic. I spent a lot of time in the house with my mom, cooking or washing dishes. When I was a freshman in high school, I did tell my folks that I wanted to go out for football. They were concerned that I would get hurt and gently suggested that I get a job in the afternoons instead. I probably couldn't have made the team anyway, so I got a job at Kroger's after school.

The income from Kroger's gave me some spending money. Since my job didn't take all my free time and with a little money in my pocket, I became a ladies' man. I found myself invited to the parties the kids were giving and became an instant convert to "Spin the Bottle," "Wink," "Post Office," and other early teen kissing games.

Dad and Polly were like all parents in wanting to know who I was with and when I was coming home. If it were someone from the church, they were, generally, more willing to let me go. A party held by any of the church kids was usually okay.

Occasionally, we were invited for dinner to the home of some friends of my folks. There was a daughter my age. While the adults were having dessert or talking, she and I spent a lot of time alone. I was developing a certain looseness of conduct that was to become increasingly serious as I grew older. Already, I was forming some habits that were to result in great difficulty in later years. I suppose most other kids went through the same kind of growing pains that I did. But my desire for attention and my deceptions to my parents and to myself left me with a mixture of increasing resentment and guilt.

My freshman year in high school and my dad's pastorate in Dayton came to a close together. He accepted the call to the Park Place Church of God in Anderson, and we left Dayton.

CHAPTER 3

In And Out Of College

I had always liked being in the spotlight, and at Anderson I finally found the perfect stage. In Dayton, a city of 250,000, it wasn't all that important being the son of the Church of God pastor. But it was different in Anderson.

The town's population was only about fifty thousand people, but there were thirteen Church of God congregations. Park Place was the largest and most prestigious due to its location on the edge of the Anderson College campus. It was also just across the street from the General Headquarters of The Church of God and Warner Press, the denomination's publishing house. I had a special status all over town and at the college, and I enjoyed every minute of it. I became a real showboat. Everybody knew that I was Dr. Dale Oldham's son.

In Dayton, I had had conflict from running around with non-church kids which made the rules and standards of the church difficult to explain. But, in Anderson, there were many kids around the church and the college who were subject to the same rules and were always ready to join me in breaking them.

I could hardly wait until I was sixteen to take the test and get my driver's license. When the day came, I was like any other kid impatiently waiting for my turn in the family car.

Then a miracle happened—or it seemed so to me at the time. Old Mrs. Pfender, a staunch member of Dad's congregation in Dayton, had always been extra-nice to me. When she died and her will was read, to my great surprise, she had left me $200.00. Dad and Polly let me use the money to buy a Model A Ford. My own car gave me the run of the town and surrounding countryside.

Since my folks didn't want me to dress in jeans like the other high-school kids, I went all out in the other direction. Dad let me get some of his old suits altered to fit me, and I was about the only kid in school who wore a dark suit, shirt and tie to school, topped off with a Homburg. I must have been a strange sight driving my Model A down the streets of Anderson.

The music teacher at Anderson High School was an attractive and talented lady named Betty Hubbard. She probably was as influential as anyone in guiding the direction of my life toward a career in music. When I was a sophomore, she encouraged me to try out for the choral club. I think I was selected largely because of her confidence in me. The next year, she suggested that I audition for the select twelve-voice group in school known as the Madrigal Club. It was a big thing to be a part of this group. Mrs. Hubbard also helped me develop a program of my own which we named "Come to the Fair." The program included some light Sigmund Romberg songs, and I gave it before several women's and service clubs in the area.

My other real interest during my junior and senior years was radio. My father had been on the radio in Dayton during the war. A government regulation made it necessary for his messages to be submitted in advance so that they could be cleared before the program. The "censor" at the station was Don Cogley. Since there was nothing subversive in the West Third Street Church of God pastor's sermons, there was never anything to delete. Nonetheless, he was required to read them and became convicted by the truth and accepted Christ.

Don was now manager of WCBC, the Christian station in Anderson. He put me on the air three times a week with a program called *High School Notes.* Good acceptance among the kids resulted in expanding the time to fifteen minutes. Radio was in my blood by then, and I was at the station almost every waking hour that I wasn't in school. By the time I was a senior, I was up early to put the station on the air at sunup. After school, I worked until sundown when it went off the air. I also did the announcing on Sundays. I kept the Model A warm driving between home, school and the radio station— Homburg and all.

Although I wasn't particularly ready, it soon became time for college and some type of decision as to where I would go and what I would study. There was never much thought about going anywhere but Anderson College. I could live at home, and I already knew most of the professors and many of the students. Choosing a major was something else.

With my Dad being such a strong preacher and leader, there were those in the church who would have liked to have "called me to preach." They hoped that I would take undergraduate work that would prepare me for the seminary and the ministry. Although I admired my Dad, I never did seriously consider being a preacher. I wasn't ready to lead a life that was open for all to see, and I still resented the long hours that he had spent away from home in his pastoral duties.

I talked with Val Clear, a sociology professor at the school who helped point me toward psychology. The subject interested me because I thought it might help me better understand myself. I wasn't quite the happy, exuberant, confidant young man that I wanted people to think. There were deep misgivings. I knew I was not only failing to measure up to my parents' expectations of me, but many of the things I did were in opposition of my own convictions.

In most ways, college wasn't a lot different from the high-school days. I swapped the Model A for a 1935 Plymouth coupe and later traded for a 1937 Studebaker coupe which

I dubbed "The Black Widow." I still wore the suits and the hat, with the addition of cowboy boots which probably made me more outlandish-looking than ever.

Again, singing captured my interest and I sang in the college choir, making the Easter vacation concert trips twice while I was at Anderson. I was taking voice lessons also, and Prof Nicholson gave me a short solo part on the hymn "My Soul Is Satisfied." It was a kind of turning-point for me. I wanted to excel and to impress the professor and the whole choir with my interpretation of the twenty-five words that were mine alone to sing. I worked on the phrasing and the word pictures like nothing I had ever done. On the choir trip, I tried each night to get more and more out of those few lines . . .

Can a bird drink up the ocean,
thirsting still from shore to shore
or the God of all creation
leave thy heart yet thirsting more . . .

I'm sure now that almost everybody knew me well enough to realize that I was showing off, but for the first time I became conscious of the different meanings that can be pulled from a set of lyrics even if I was doing it with the wrong motive. My interest in singing grew from that moment on.

My enthusiasm mounted when I was chosen to be a member of The Christian Brotherhood Hour staff quartet. A couple of years before, my father and Dick Lee, now a Los Angeles radio producer, had started the program with a network of sixteen stations. The idea, originally, had been to bring in a different minister every three months. However, Dad was the first speaker, and it was twenty-one years before he retired and was replaced.

The quartet was organized in 1949 and included Lowell Williamson, Homer Shower, Gene Dyer and myself. I was the only freshman; the others were juniors and seniors. The network had greatly expanded by the time the quartet was formed, and it was heady stuff to know my voice was being heard by all those people "out in radioland." We made our first recording on the Tru-Tone label and were doubly proud as the McGuire Sisters were also on the label.

A summer tour proved to be the most enjoyable venture of all. The Brotherhood Hour offered to underwrite our expenses and pay us a small fee as well. But we had the old college confidence and decided we could do better if we handled it ourselves. So we wrote some letters and arranged our own booking.

Lowell had a new Chevy, and we agreed to pay him seven cents a mile while on the tour. We jammed everything, including sound systems, clothes and records, into his car and headed west for a summer of nearly eighty concerts in sixty-nine days in Illinois, Iowa, Nebraska, Oklahoma and Kansas. At the end of the summer, we had each earned around $135 a week. This amount not only tripled what we had been offered but enabled us to pay our tuition for the coming year. I think God was gently leading me into my lifework, although I didn't realize it at the time. I only knew that music, traveling, recording, concerts and churches were becoming more and more important to me.

My tuition costs were assured, but my academic standing was something else. The main problem was that I didn't go to class. If anybody wanted to go anywhere or do anything, I would cut class even if it meant missing an important test. It wasn't long before my grades reflected my poor attendance. Then, I was continually getting crossed up with the administration. I suspect I had the feeling that nothing was going to happen to Dr. Dale Oldham's son.

I was a little ahead of the times maybe, but I was an angry young man and a leader in griping about the faculty and school. During my freshman year, the school had conducted a fund-raising campaign to build a dorm for the ministerial students. After the goal was reached, there was some crisis which resulted in a decision to build a girls' dorm first. Now, I really didn't care all that much whether the ministerial students had a new dorm or not. But it was a popular issue on campus among the students, and I jumped right into the middle of it. One afternoon, when the student center was about half full, I managed to engage some of the faculty in a discussion of the matter. I talked loudly enough to attract most of the students. Strengthened by my sympathetic audience, I said some very harsh things about the dean and the administration.

A couple of days later, Dean Horton called me into her office to discuss both the incident and my grades. She tried to be as diplomatic as possible, but she was quite firm. We reached a mutual agreement that it would be better both for the school and for me if I went to college somewhere else.

Somewhere else was Hanover College in southern Indiana—150 miles from Anderson—where I enrolled in the fall of 1950. I was not prepared for the shock that came! Not long after I had made my first drive up the winding road past the athletic field to my dorm, just short of the quadrangle, I realized a disturbing fact: no one knew who I was! Furthermore, they couldn't have cared less. This revelation was quite a come-down for a former big-man-on-campus. At Hanover, no one had ever heard of Dale Oldham, much less me.

My response to this anonymity was to ignore the school, too. After three or four weeks, I quit going to classes—period. I didn't cut classes—I simply quit. My preoccupation was with sleep. I usually slept until two or three o'clock in the afternoon. Then, I'd get up, shower, shave and dress to meet some friends (Clayburn Quinn was one of my buddies). We'd talk until dinnertime, after which I'd either find a date or go back to my room and read until bedtime. Some days I was sleeping up to sixteen hours.

After a few weeks, my psychology professor, "Doc" Zirkle, called me into his office. When I got there, I hardly recognized him in his tie and suit. I seldom saw him in anything but a sweat suit, jogging through the quad. Now, sitting behind his desk, he seemed out of place. Scratching his graying temples, he studied the book in front of him, then said, "We have come to midterm and with the exception of the first couple of weeks, I don't have anything in my grade book for you. Don't you like psychology?"

"Oh, I like it a lot," I replied.

"Well, why don't you come to class?"

Since I didn't have an answer, he continued: "I have a feeling you should be getting A's, but unless you do something in a hurry, you're going to fail. We are at the point of no return. If you work hard the rest of the term, you salvage a decent grade. But if you're going to continue in the same pattern, I'd suggest you go home now. There is just no use wasting the time or the money."

I decided to give it a try, and for the remainder of the term I worked hard, pulling my grades up as Professor Zirkle had promised. However, when the semester ended, I packed up my clothes, my tennis racket, my bedding; threw away my pipes (I'd taken up smoking, privately) and went home. I didn't tell anyone I was leaving, and I didn't tell anyone I was coming. I was just tired of the place. The fact that no one knew me was a real drain on my ego. So I went back to Anderson—home base—and asked to be reinstated.

"I'm ready to work this time," I said. Either they believed me, or Dad wielded his influence, because I was readmitted to class. By now, though, the folks were beginning to see that I was either very poorly adjusted or just plain egotistical and spoiled.

I was so glad to be back in Anderson that I had serious intentions about making good my promise to work. It wasn't long, however, until something happened that was to point out two things: first, that I really hadn't changed much, and second, that my parents' attitude *had* changed.

It was a minor scrape in comparison with some of my escapades, but the result was devastating. After breaking the windshield on a friend's car, Dad was as tough as he had ever been with me. He simply refused to pay for it and informed me that I would have to get a job and earn the money myself.

The obvious place to start looking for a job was at the big Delco Remy plant where lots of fellows from school worked the 3:30 P.M. to 1:00 A.M. shift. It was with a great deal of hurt pride and anger that I got into the employment line with some fifty other guys. I would show my Dad that I could get along without his help. By the look on most of the faces of the boys coming out of the office, not many were being hired. I thought about leaving but my pride was at stake, so I waited. When my turn came, I found that the interviewer was a friend of my Dad's. He gave me a job as a night inspector which was easy enough. I sat on a stool watching condensers roll by on a conveyor belt and, occasionally, rejected one that had a bad weld. The money was good and it wasn't long before I had paid for the windshield.

Meanwhile, I had fallen back into the same old pattern at school. I lacked the dedication of some of the other guys who worked the same shift and kept up their school load as well. I excused myself on the grounds of being too exhausted and began to miss classes again. Even worse, I began cutting chapel.

On a small Christian college campus, great pains are taken by the administration to insure attendance at chapel. Chapel at Anderson was held on Monday, Wednesday and Friday at 10:15. Seats were assigned and the attendance was taken by 10:20. If your seat was empty, you were given a chapel cut. You were allowed only five for the term, and for each additional cut, two percent was deducted from your grades. With my poor attendance in class, it didn't take long for my grades to begin their usual plummet below the passing mark.

Although I hadn't kept up with classes or chapel at either school, I had been very regular in dating. I knew the town, had a car and generally managed to date anyone I asked. I had the happy faculty—or the unhappy one—of falling in love quite often and deeply. Soon, I had a steady girl at Anderson, and we began to discuss marriage. At Christmas break, she planned to go home to discuss possible engagement arrangements with her parents.

However, I suddenly began to notice Laura Lee Makings on the campus. I learned her name from a friend. Then, I remembered that she was the one for whom the student body had taken a collection so she could return home for her father's funeral. She sang in the choir at our church, and I told Polly, one day, that she was the girl I was going to marry. I remember Polly saying, candidly, "Well, Doug, she isn't pretty, but she keeps herself neat." I must not have been looking at the same girl, because her sunny smile and warm, brown eyes affected me differently.

Laura knew me from the times I had sung in chapel and at church. Later, she told me that although she liked to hear me sing, she felt that I was a somewhat troubled person and she had enough troubles of her own. So, she gave me a wide berth and, occasionally, would miss chapel if she knew I was going to sing.

One beautiful, snowy evening during the Christmas holidays changed all that for both of us.

CHAPTER 4
Laura

In a way Anderson was a lonely place during Christmas. Most of the students had gone home for the holidays. But in the quiet of the nearly empty dorms and student center, there was also a kind of bond among those who had stayed behind. One of those people was Laura Lee Makings, who simply could not afford to make the trip home.

There was a lovely snow, and the town was covered in a quiet, white blanket. The choir from the church was going caroling in the neighborhood nearby. The Park Place section of Anderson is made up of gracious old homes with small, neat yards, sidewalks and stately, old trees. That night, it looked like a Norman Rockwell painting.

I don't remember who else was there, but I do remember, before we were halfway through the neighborhood, I was walking with Laura. After the caroling was over and we had been to the sponsor's house for hot chocolate, I asked if I could take her home. We stopped outside the town at the Red Brick Inn for a sandwich and played the jukebox. It was a lovely night. I can still remember the cold, night air outside and the warm excitement I felt within.

Laura and I went out together once more during the holidays before the other students, including my girlfriend, returned

to the campus. Polly arranged an outing one afternoon following a deep snow. The four of us—Dad, Polly, Laura and I—took
a walk in the snowy woods outside of town before supper.

It wasn't long before my other romance died a natural death,
and I began to date Laura in earnest.

Thinking back, we can recall only a few "formal" dates
that winter. One was a class party when I gave Laura a camellia
corsage. Another time we went to a Booster Club formal at
the Top Hat. I gave her my club pin which was supposed
to mean we were going steady. Laura wasn't quite ready for
everyone to know she was that serious about me, so she pinned
it to her slip.

We had our share of lovers' quarrels. When I returned from
the spring choir tour, I learned that she had dated somebody
else while I was away. I created a big scene which was the
forerunner of many others to come in our relationship.

Of course, we saw each other often at church and church-
related functions, but we were too busy to do much else. We
both went to school part of the day and worked the rest. I
was still working the same shift at Delco Remy, and Laura
was working at the beauty shop from 1:00 to 7:00 P.M., earning
money to stay in school. Then, she helped out at the Nicholsons
in return for her room and board, after which she studied
for the next day's classes. If the light was still on in her first-
floor bedroom when I drove home from work, I'd stop by
to talk through the window screen. Sometimes we'd talk an
hour or more. I can still remember those metallic goodnight
kisses.

From the very first, Laura had me figured pretty well. I
became dizzy one night at work and was brought home and
put to bed. Polly feared the worst, and I happily stayed in
bed for two or three days, thoroughly enjoying the attention
and the rest. When Laura Lee came by to see me, she saw
through the game I was playing and said, "You're sick all
right—sick in the head. You ought to be ashamed." With that,
she left.

Suddenly, I regretted that I was bedridden and rushed to the window. She had not yet left the walk to turn west toward Seventh Street.

"Laura, I still love you," I called, feverishly.

She stopped, thought earnestly for a moment, took a deep breath and then dropped her shoulders in resignation. Reversing her steps, she returned to the house where we made up. That was the turning-point for Laura who had been seriously considering breaking up with me for good. I was such a complicated person that she just wasn't sure she wanted to undertake such a project.

By spring, our love had deepened. There was a stability and depth about Laura which I thought would help to settle me down. Since the people in our church didn't believe in wearing rings, I bought her a watch to make our engagement official. Dad made the formal announcement of our engagement at an all-school Booster Club program in the late spring, and we set the date for November 30, 1951, my twenty-first birthday!

In the summer when school was out, we accompanied my parents west as far as Trenton, Nebraska—population, 921— where I spent a week with Laura and her mother while Dad spoke at a camp meeting in Colorado. It was an interesting and revealing week, because I learned a great deal about my future wife's background.

Laura's family, the Weaver Makings, were real-for-sure homesteaders. Dad Makings and a brother worked a large spread in Park County, seventy miles west of Colorado Springs. It was a tough life, with everybody pitching in for long, fourteen-hour days to provide only the bare necessities.

The one-room cabin was heated by a wood stove and lit by kerosene lamps. There was no indoor plumbing. It was a strange contrast to my comfortable, middle-class upbringing. I had always been surrounded by people and attention, but Laura had had few social experiences. Our religious backgrounds were very different, too. Whereas I had grown up in a highly religious atmosphere, her family did not attend church at all. Her Dad thought it was a waste of time, and time was a luxury they could not afford. The ranch required a seven-day workweek.

Laura remembers going to church only twice in her first sixteen years. Once was to a funeral and the other was to Bible School. A neighbor, concerned about the Makings kids' religious education, volunteered to take them to church during the two-week school, but Laura and her cousin attended only one day. They didn't like it and the next day hid down by the creek under the bridge until the neighbor drove off for Bible School without them.

Theirs was a close family filled with genuine caring for each other. This concern spread throughout the sparsely-peopled community. The nearest town, Hartzel, with a population of about one hundred, was seventeen miles away, and it was over a mile to the nearest neighbor's house. The harsh realities of life were always present, and one of Laura's most vivid recollections is of the death of a neighbor boy when she was about ten.

On her way home from school one day, Laura got out of a neighbor's car with her cousin and Walter Spencer, whose family lived nearest to the Makings. Each day, the three of them would walk part of the way home together, then cut across the fields in separate directions. On this particular day, a violent storm arose suddenly and caught the children in the open. When they came to the place in the field where their paths parted, they waved goodbye and each ran toward home. Just seconds after they separated, lightning struck. When the girls turned, Walter was nowhere to be seen. He had been hit by the bolt. Laura's dad carried his tattered clothing home, and it lay outside the backdoor for several days as a grim reminder of their constant struggle with nature.

Tragedy came even closer to home during Christmas of the same year. The long hours and rigorous work caught up with her father, and he suffered a massive heart attack. He was rushed to the veterans' hospital in Denver, where he lingered near death for many months. Finally, he recovered enough to move to Nebraska. When it became certain that he could never go back to work again, the hard-pressed family had to make other arrangements. Laura went to live with an aunt who also lived in Nebraska. She was a devout Christian who attended the Church of God. It was here that Laura started regular church attendance for the first time in her life. Eventually, she gave her heart to Christ and decided to attend the church-sponsored college at Anderson, Indiana. Her father, who still had no time for the church, was displeased and told her, "If you go to that church school, don't bother to come home." Although she didn't know it when she left for school, Laura would never see her father alive again. In September, 1950, with $80.00 in her pocket, she arrived at school, short of almost everything except faith and a strong-willed independence which she had gained from her life on the ranch.

The trip across the Midwest was beautiful, and when my folks dropped us off in Laura's hometown, we found her mother working as a cook in a restaurant. We borrowed her Chevrolet to drive around and visit some of Laura's old friends, one of whom was her old boss in the beauty shop. I found Grace, her mother, to be as straightforward and disarming as Laura. A strong woman who had been dealt some heavy blows in life, she had persevered. She knew that Laura and I were considering marriage, so she spent a good part of the time sizing me up. Though Laura didn't tell me about it at the time, her mother told her that she liked me "despite the fact that I was a very self-centered person." Like Laura Lee, Mrs. Makings was a good judge of character.

When we returned to Anderson, the plans for the wedding were begun. Since I was merely the groom, I had no idea how much planning was involved in a wedding. This one had all the usual complications and some others, too, as it turned out. Laura's mother certainly didn't have the money to finance a big church wedding, and Laura was working to pay her way through college. She felt it would have to be a simple ceremony. Polly and Dad felt strongly that the family owed it to the church to have a large church wedding so that everyone could come. The folks insisted on paying all the expenses, so Laura reluctantly agreed.

Polly, of course, had had vast experience in helping with the weddings that Dad had conducted over the many years he had been a pastor. Laura, I doubt, had ever been to a formal church wedding. She was new in town, broke, working and going to school. Polly wanted to help and plunged right in. Together, they picked the wedding gown, the bridesmaid's dress, the flowers, the invitations, the cake and attended to all the other details. But Polly, strong and confident in her role as pastor's wife, overshadowed the quiet, farm girl and ended up making most of the decisions.

She had certainly planned well. The wedding was an affair that saw the pastor's only son married in proper style. Maurice Berquist was the best man and Mary Freebe, the maid of honor. Laura's mother came for the occasion. The church was packed and the music was especially selected. There was a trend at that time to use newer, secular songs that had special significance for the bride and groom, but this was carefully avoided at our wedding. I sang "Be My Love," but the lyrics were "spiritualized" so as to be appropriate, and Laura sang "All For You." As we knelt following the vows, Marie Lynn played "Saviour, Like a Shepherd Lead Us" softly on the violin, while Dad prayed. It was a lovely song with deep meaning for my Dad. This meaning, added to the solemnity of the occasion, inspired him to pray a "filibuster." I thought my knees would break before he finished.

There was a huge reception afterward, and we opened gifts until 11:30. The moment finally arrived when we slipped away for our honeymoon trip of forty miles and three days in faraway Indianapolis.

When we returned, we moved into Grandma Oldham's apartment with our hundreds of wedding gifts. Grandma Oldham had gone to live with a daughter, and we inherited the old furniture from her own newly-married days. Laura and I resumed school and work, and we lived happily ever after. Well, not quite.

There were a few bumps. On the first night after returning to our school-work schedule, Laura came home from the beauty parlor with visions of preparing her first succulent meal. It was to be homemade vegetable soup. Canned soup was certainly not good enough for her new husband.

When she finished her Epicurean delight, she tasted it. The vegetables on the bottom were burned, while other bits of charred celery and carrots floated on top. In desperation, she called Polly, who was more than willing to help her son's new bride. When she got to our place, the problem was solved in an instant. The solution was to throw the soup out and start over—this time, adding meat.

"Meat in vegetable soup?" Laura Lee asked, incredulously.

"Yes, it gives it more body," Polly informed her.

And so, Laura learned her first culinary trick: vegetable soup needs meat.

When we'd been married a month or so, Polly dropped in to visit. She took one look at the untidy house and gasped. Immaculate herself, she thought Laura's housekeeping left something to be desired. Dad and I were enlisted and soon had the place shipshape.

"Laura Lee's just too busy going to school and working to do the housework the way she'd like to do it," Polly told us.

We scrubbed and dusted and swept and straightened all afternoon. I thought it was nice of her and Dad to be so interested. I did not anticipate Laura's reaction.

When she came home from the beauty shop, she looked at the house coolly and thanked Polly with no trace of annoyance. But after they had gone home, Laura spoke her piece to me. Polly had been picking up after me for as long as I could remember, so I couldn't understand the fuss.

The next time Polly came by to help, she asked how Laura was doing on the wedding gift thank-you notes. This seems to be a matter of gravest importance to all mothers of brides and grooms. Laura said that she hadn't begun. "Mercy!" said Polly, or words to that effect. The next day, Polly sent a girl over to write them for Laura. Since she was hiring a girl to write the notes that she had bought to thank the people whom she had invited to the wedding, it seemed appropriate enough that Laura now referred to the whole thing as "Polly's wedding." It was the beginning of a resentment that was to plague Laura for a long time. It was to surface much later, compounded with many other problems.

CHAPTER 5
An Accusation

Not long after Laura's thank-you notes were in the mail, the postman brought me a note from the dean of students requesting that I report to the office. I knew what it was about. My grades had hit an all-time low. I was failing everything but chapel, and I had quit attending there. In the eyes of the administration, that seemed to be worse than failure in a regular class.

"It's not that you aren't capable of the work, Doug," the registrar said on the day I went to face the music. "You aren't applying yourself. I just can't figure it out. But until you make up your mind to study, I think you're wasting your time here." She didn't come right out and say I was expelled from school, but I understood pretty well what she meant.

And I was ready to do something different. Strangely enough, though, with the exception of my interests in radio and singing, I didn't have much of an idea what I wanted to do in life. As long as I was in college I could postpone the decision, but an abrupt dismissal from school called for some immediate plans. I wasn't ready for that. Many of the kids in our town went straight from high school to Delco Remy and settled there for life. I knew that wasn't for me. But I was ready to leave the responsibilities of college that I had

taken so lightly and escape from the small town where everyone knew me so well. I needed a fresh start.

I left the administration building and went directly to Dad's
study at the church. It wasn't easy to break the news to him.
To my surprise, there was no lecture. Instead, he had a very
practical suggestion. Dad had talked to Prof Nicholson earlier
in the day and had learned of an opening for a minister of
music at the First Church of God in High Point, North Carolina. The minister was Arlo Newell, a graduate of Anderson,
who had attended Park Place. He had been a campus leader
when I was in high school.

"Maybe he could use you. Does the idea interest you?" It
didn't, really, but I wanted out, and it was a door.

"If you are, go and see Professor Nicholson and he'll give
you Arlo's phone number."

Before the morning was over, I had called High Point and
talked with Arlo. Although the church was small and could
not afford to pay me a salary, he was certain they could find
a job for me. If she wanted it, there was a job waiting for
Laura Lee in the knitting mills. I told him we would come
as soon as possible, but even I didn't realize how soon that
was going to be.

My next stop was to the beauty shop. When I asked Laura
how she would like to live south of the Mason-Dixon line,
she replied like a ridiculously obedient bride of two months,

"Oh, fine." I really think she was trying to remember where
the Mason-Dixon line was—aside from being the name of a
trucking company.

"I think they're getting ready to kick me out of Anderson
for the second time, and I guess maybe we would be smart
to go."

"Go where?"

"To North Carolina. A church has asked me to come and
help with the music. There is a job waiting for you, and I
could enroll in some college classes along with my work at
the church."

With no more thought than that, we both quit school, and Laura quit her job. That very same afternoon, Dad bought us a car for $300.00, we rented a trailer, packed our belongings (which had been unpacked only a short time) and pulled out in the early hours of the morning. It was just like leaving Hanover College. When I was ready to move, it didn't take long to get going.

We were almost groggy from the events that had transpired so quickly, but we were young and excited about starting out on our own. We had only $135.00 for the trip, most of which had been given to us by one of the guys in the quartet, Lowell Williamson. We decided to drive straight through, stopping only long enough to eat and rest a little.

It was February, and we soon hit February weather. About two or three o'clock in the morning on a winding mountain road, we were struck by a terrific wind and knew by the weather reports that we were approaching a storm. Our open trailer was crammed with new, mostly unused wedding gifts and clothes. We were both scared and tired and, as a few drops of rain hit the windshield, Laura began to pray. I was frantically looking for a place to take cover—a barn, a garage, anything. Laura had barely finished her prayer when we topped a huge hill. Just on the other side was a filling station, blazing with light. I pulled in under the large, covered driveway. The attendant came out to see what we needed just as the clouds broke loose.

I felt foolish as I asked him, "I don't suppose you have anything that would cover our trailer?"

"It just so happens I do have a tarpaulin—and I'll sell it to you cheap."

It was just the right size. With his help, we secured it with rope and were on our way a few minutes later. Our purse was $40.00 lighter, but we were certain that it had not been a coincidence that we had found the filling station, the tarp and the rope at exactly the moment we needed it.

For the rest of the trip I fell in behind a truck that was

hurtling along at high speed and followed him through the rain, sleet and fog. It probably wasn't the safest thing to do, but it got us there.

The only other incident on the trip was Laura's car-sickness. I don't think I ever saw anybody quite so sick for quite so long.

It was early morning by the time we drove through the rolling Piedmont countryside in central North Carolina into High Point, a town of about forty thousand. The storm was over, and it was cold and clear. Maybe, here was our place of beginning again.

Arlo and his wife, Helen, had found us a place to live just outside of High Point. They helped us move our things up the steps into the second-floor apartment of the gray, frame building. The owner lived on the ground floor, and our apartment had just two rooms—a living room which doubled as a bedroom and the kitchen. There was a half-bath in the hall at the top of the stairs, but you had to go downstairs to take a shower. You also had to chase the black widows and scorpions out of the tub. The apartment also had a fuel-oil stove that didn't hold enough oil to get through a day or night. We carried oil constantly, it seemed. The house was old and showed plenty of wear. The brown linoleum was badly worn in several spots, and the floors were warped so badly that anything that was dropped in the room rolled toward the middle. There were no cupboards in the kitchen, and the sink was chipped and ugly. But we planned to move as soon as we both found jobs—and had a paycheck or two.

The folks at the church had been able to find a job for Laura in the textile mills, but she still wasn't feeling well enough to take it. The illness that had first shown up on the trip from Anderson hung on mysteriously. In fact, Laura went to bed almost as soon as we had finished moving in, and she just couldn't get up. I began to wonder if it was something more serious. I would have taken her to a doctor right away, but we were strapped for money. I had discussed her sickness with Arlo every day, and he was greatly concerned. He came by to see if she was feeling better quite often. On one occasion, I had a request.

"Arlo, when you pray today, will you ask God to rebuke Laura Lee's affliction?"

He read a verse or two from the Scriptures and we knelt to pray. I waited for him to ask the Lord to eliminate the source of this illness, but he made no mention of it. When we stepped out on the porch at the end of his visit, I asked Arlo why he had not prayed about Laura's health. He smiled and suggested something that had never crossed our minds.

"Helen and I were talking last night," Arlo said, "and we think Laura Lee might be expecting."

Almost in unison, we exclaimed, "A baby!" Why hadn't we thought of it? It had never dawned on us. I was an only child raised in a nice, neat pastor's home far removed from births and deaths and crying babies. Laura was raised on an isolated homestead with one brother who was eight years older than she. From then on, morning sickness would have a greater significance in our lives.

This made me the sole breadwinner in the family, and I was floored. I was going to have to get a job, go to school, work in the church and take care of Laura. And she was asking for things like lemon pie, grape pop and homemade vegetable soup. The apartment was cluttered with unpacked boxes. I had never even been on my own, except for the quarter I spent at Hanover College. To top it all, I was to be a father. The responsibilities of life had descended on me all at once. I settled down to carrying fuel day and night, eating grocery poundcake and drinking milk. No dirty dishes that way.

I found a job as a disc jockey on WPHE working the night shift. The station was owned by the same people who owned

the newspaper, *The Enterprise,* and was located over the newspaper office on the second floor. Since it was air-conditioned,
I looked forward to going to work on hot, summer nights.

One of my jobs at the station, occasionally, was to put the
Christian Brotherhood Hour on the air. The program was
recorded and came into the station on discs. It was a strange
feeling cueing up the record, turning up the pot and sending
my dad's voice out over the air. It made me homesick for
Anderson and the program, especially now that it was on 350
stations across the country.

With my experience in the business, I could handle the job
easily as far as ability was concerned. But it seemed I couldn't
handle my emotions. I got into an argument with the station
manager, and he asked me to turn in my earphones. This
was a blow, since we needed the money so badly.

We were so low on cash at one time that I couldn't afford
to have a flat tire fixed. Clyde Ward, who was a contractor
and a member of the church, stopped by the house one night
and noticed that the car was jacked up.

"What's the problem?" he asked.

"Just a flat," I told him.

"Well, throw it in the trunk. We'll take it down to the corner
station."

When I told him I had planned to wait until Saturday, he
said, "Why wait? That's the day after tomorrow."

"To tell the truth, I'm broke."

He laughed. "Well, why didn't you say so." And with that,
he threw the tire into the trunk, drove me to the station and
paid the $1.50. It was not the only time he was to help us.

After the radio stint, I signed up for a selling program school
at Sears. The school was fine, but I ran into problems right
away when it came time to get the name on the line for the
vacuum cleaner. Next, I got tremendously excited about
Knight and Bostwick's landscaping school. They had an excellent training program and hundreds of beautiful shrubs.

But, since the trick was to get them into someone's yard, prepaid, that venture fizzled out, also. As a salesman, I was a total failure.

Finally, a job opened at the Silver Knit Hosiery Mills. Guy Kinney, a fine Sunday School teacher and personnel director for the company, asked me if I wanted to learn to knit. I was really pleased to have the opportunity. A knitting job paid about $90.00 a week at that time and was a coveted position. I became a qualified Comet machine operator, eventually working my way up to more than a dozen units at once. In other words, I was able to produce up to 144 dozen pairs of men's socks in an eight-hour shift.

But it was an exhausting job—one which required great concentration and fast reflexes. When a sock is finished, the operator has three or four seconds to snip three threads, pull one thread, remove the sock, reverse it over his arm and throw the finished sock over his shoulder. Snip, pull, reverse, flip . . . snip, pull, reverse, flip—all night long. One other problem was the heat. Because we used nylon thread, the mill was not air-conditioned, so I often worked in temperatures up to 110 degrees or more. The air was so full of lint, my nostrils felt as if I had Q-tips in them.

The job was also nerve-wracking. An operator could take thirty minutes to eat, but he seldom had relief, so his work would pile up while he was away. The machines never stopped running, so he would spend the rest of the shift trying to catch up. After awhile, I settled for one of Rex Skidmore's chili dogs and a Coke. Rex was a member of our church and ran a food cart at the plant. I'd eat standing up so I wouldn't get so far behind. Those were the best chili dogs with cheese I ever tasted.

It didn't take long for the situation at High Point to begin to deteriorate for me. In the first place, I had been used to other people worrying and fussing over me. I didn't know how to help other people with their problems because I had always been so preoccupied with my own. And, certainly, Laura needed help during those months at High Point. She was expecting and sick and stuck in the hot, little house into which we had moved from the apartment. The house was not air-conditioned and the oatbugs came through the screens.

At night while I was at work, Laura was too nervous to sleep. I had bought her a little Pomeranian dog that she named "Duchess." Thanks to Duchess, Laura could sleep a little knowing the dog would bark its head off if anyone came near the window. She really loved Duchess and often walked her on a leash, since the traffic moved very fast on the street in front of the house. I was too lazy to walk her and just let her run free. One day, a car struck her while I was sitting on the porch. Laura cried for a solid week, with little sympathy from me. It was typical of my insensitivity to her.

By now I could barely face life. I worked on the night shift and slept most of the day.

Fortunately, the work at the church was not very demanding. There was a rehearsal on Thursday nights and the services on Sundays. I was inexperienced and probably worked the choir harder than was necessary, but they responded and the people appreciated the music. However, I was beginning to have other problems in the church.

There is a very strict line of propriety that must be observed by members of a church staff. Ministers, especially, must be very careful to hold themselves above even the faintest suspicion. They can easily become victims of circumstances and must use caution in visiting in homes and in their conduct with female parishioners.

Partly because of the habits I had formed in high school and college, and partly because of a desire for attention that Laura was not feeling well enough to give me, I was not very careful. I left myself wide open to criticism. In fact, I revelled in the attention and generally walked as close to the edge as I possibly could, not realizing I was courting disaster. This included playing favorites among lady choir members and taking unescorted female members home after practice. I thought that I had drawn the line in my own mind, but I flirted openly and often, inviting the criticism of the church.

The city was small, and the church was a closely knit family. It soon became a regular procedure for Arlo to have to defend my actions to various individuals in the church and on the board. I shrugged off his counsel and condemned the church as a group of over-critical people. But by now I was in deep, spiritual trouble. I had crossed the line in my mind, and my flirting and teasing began to take on a different flavor. It was only a matter of time until the place and the person would present themselves at the appropriate time. I had gone too far. All of these activities were merely a prelude to the affair that followed.

After the choir rehearsals, I had begun to visit the house of one of the choir members. It had started innocently enough at the time, but had I been spiritually alert, I would have realized that I was skating on thin ice. I had genuinely hoped that marrying Laura would settle me down and put me on the track spiritually. But we had not had much time to develop a strong relationship. The move, the poor living conditions, and the frustrations of finding a job, as well as her miserable sickness, left me feeling trapped and discouraged. I was a perfect candidate for someone who would inflate my ego and lend an understanding ear.

Yet, I knew the things I was doing would destroy Laura if she found out, and I was overcome with guilt. Time after time, I would resolve not to go again, but I could never find the strength to carry them through. It was not the first time, nor was it to be the last, before I finally came to the place where I could let God change me.

Mine is not an easy story to tell, and I cannot bring myself, even now, to relate the details. It isn't a bright, happy, romantic story, and I feel only shame and disgust at what I was. But the richness of God's mercy can be shown most clearly in contrast to the shabbiness and sordidness of a soul.

My heart and life were such a mess, it was to be years before it was all straightened out. Although Laura was a genuine Christian, she hadn't lived long enough to know how to help us. And, since she didn't even know what we were fighting, her despair was almost akin to mine. It seemed the devil was out to finish us off right then and there. And he very nearly did.

Lord help us, we were to become parents momentarily. Babies don't wait for you to grow up—they just come anyway. We called Laura's mother who dutifully came—the first of many times.

In mid-October, Laura, Mrs. Makings and I were downtown when the pains began. About six o'clock in the evening, we admitted Laura to the hospital. At precisely 12:01 A.M., October 15, 1952, I became the father of an eight-pound daughter who was born looking at the world with black, flashing, defiant eyes. She was to live with trouble and anxiety having full play around her. When I see her today—wise, witty, full of Christian grace and principle—I only know that somebody was praying all the time I was failing, and that God is not deaf.

The pressures at the church were rapidly coming to a climax. When you do wrong, you go to sleep at night and you wake up in the morning fearing that this is the day you'll be found out. Sure enough, the day came and the meeting was called. Again, I was at a crossroads. It was time to face up and come clean, to ask God's forgiveness, to be honest with the pastor and the church—or to run, leaving a cloud of dust behind and hoping you will be in the next county before it settles.

"Dad, it's not working out down here, and I want to move," I said over the phone that afternoon.

Once again, I chose to run.

CHAPTER 6
A Familiar Pattern

Probably the last thing Laura wanted to hear was the news that we were moving. Paula was only a couple of weeks old, and Laura was barely beginning to get a little of her color and strength back. The whole nine months of her pregnancy had been so hard on her physically and mentally that I knew my news couldn't possibly meet with much enthusiasm.

I found her in the kitchen with her mother. She followed me into the bedroom where I broke the news that we were leaving. Stunned, she sank down on the bed. After hearing my explanation, she recovered her composure, put her arms around me and told me that she believed in me completely and knew the rumors were not true. Her confidence, in light of my actions, made me feel lower than ever, and I vowed once again to straighten myself up. On the spot, I prayed, "God, somehow help me to get over this hurdle. Don't let this end my service to You. Help me find another job and give me another chance. I promise that I won't ever disappoint You again."

Laura was more concerned with where we would go and how soon we would have to move. I told her not to worry—I'd work it out.

Dad had given me a couple of leads to check out, one of which was the Fifth Avenue Church of God in Huntington,

West Virginia. It proved to be the right place. They needed someone right away and asked me to drive up for an interview. Three days later, the pastor called to tell me I was hired and could begin work immediately.

The move from High Point to Huntington, West Virginia was, to all outward appearances, a promotion. It was a much larger church which paid $50 a week plus $80 a month for living quarters. We found a beautiful apartment on an estate, Dunfee Hill. It was a three-story, turn-of-the-century, red brick mansion that sat high on a pedestal of green overlooking a valley below. A winding, circular road lined by stately trees led to the breathtaking home. It was not unusual to flush out a covey of quail on the drive from the main road. On the front lawn there was a picture-book gazebo; and, in the rear, a large flower garden, attended by a professional gardener. A porch off the living room of our second-floor apartment brought the whole panorama to view in just a few steps. After the heat in High Point, this setting was a quiet, cool refuge on hot summer days.

When I told Polly and Dad that I had taken the Huntington job, they arranged to help us move. Although they were due in Miami for a national youth conference, they left Anderson a few days early to lend a hand. Laura had been getting things together for a week, though she hardly felt well enough. When Polly and Dad arrived, she mustered her courage and joined the movers.

We moved on election night, November 2, 1952—the night Eisenhower was elected to the Presidency over Stevenson. I remember hearing Mr. Stevenson's speech when he conceded the election. It described my feeling perfectly about the things that had happened in High Point and our forced move. He said, "I'm too old to cry, but it hurts to laugh."

When we finished loading, we said our goodbyes to the landlord and set out for Huntington. It was a long drive on top of an all-day packing stint, but we all agreed it would be best to "get it over with." Laura slept on the trip as much as three-week-old Paula would let her, but it was poor preparation for what lay ahead. Paula made the trip in a bureau drawer on a pillow.

When we arrived at Dunfee Hill at 3:00 A.M., the folks wanted to unpack immediately. Since they really needed to start for Miami as soon as possible, I groaned silently and began the long ordeal, grateful for their help. Laura was in no shape to lift the heavy boxes, but she was too gritty not to try. And I was too young and inconsiderate to tell her she shouldn't.

Back and forth we trudged. Up and down. I remember to this day the seventeen steps to the landing, and having to switch the load at the top to make it through the door. Finally, sometime before daybreak, we got the last box inside, and all of us fell onto mattresses, completely exhausted. The minister of music of the Fifth Avenue Church of God had arrived.

Ivan Alls was the minister. I liked him right away and felt that I would be able to work with him. He was a big guy with glasses which led one friend to call him Ivan "Owls." Ivan was young and very serious about his work. This made it a little hard, because I wasn't serious about anything. I didn't know much about the job of being minister of music anyway, and I covered up by playing everything very loose.

As a full-time staff member, I was assigned the duties of the janitor and church secretary in addition to my job as director of the choir. Ivan and I took turns making the hospital calls.

I confided to Ivan the accusations made by the folks in High Point and assured him they were unfounded. I didn't really want to be completely open about it, but I was sure that he would hear the rumors eventually, and I preferred he heard the story from me.

I got along all right at the church with few exceptions. I opened the building for meetings, closed it, cleaned it, handled

the mimeographing of bulletins, led the choir and did some
of the ministerial duties such as making house and hospital
calls. I made the calls, but I was always careful not to see
anybody. At homes, I'd knock once very lightly and leave,
praying that no one had heard my knock. I went to the hospital
at lunch time or afternoon naptime or when I was sure the
patients would have other visitors. The last thing I wanted
was to have to offer spiritual advice or counsel to someone
when I was struggling to find answers for my own prayer.
Of course, there were times when I had to lead in prayer
and to pretend deep feelings which I did not have. It was
not that I didn't believe in the Bible or its teachings. I had
just never been able to maintain any meaningful spiritual
relationship with Christ. I'd been to the altar dozens of times
as a kid, but I had always had trouble living a consistent
Christian life. This inadequacy became painfully obvious when
I was called upon to share or counsel from my own spiritual
experiences.

Being raised in the Church of God, I had been to the altar
on numerous occasions in my life. I remember very vividly
going forward in Dayton when I was twelve years old. Ross
Minkler was the evangelist. Not only was he a strong preacher
but a singer and songwriter as well. However, I remember
him best as a great storyteller. He always stayed at our house
while he was holding special services at Dad's church, and
I liked him and the funny stories he told.

One night toward the end of the meeting, I was sitting on
the left-hand side of the aisle in the second row with Polly.
She was sitting there so she could be near the organ ready
to play for the invitation.

After he asked those under conviction to make their way
to the altar, Ross began singing a song he had written:

> *Many years I'd longed for rest,*
> *Perfect peace within my breast,*
> *And I often sought the Lord*
> *In deep despair.*

But I would not pay the price,
Would not make the sacrifice,
I wandered on and on for many years.
Let me lose myself and find it, Lord, in Thee,
May all self be slain,
My friends see only Thee.
Though it cost me grief and pain,
I will find myself again,
If I lose myself
I'll find it, Lord, in Thee.

I'd been studying my shoes and the bare floor of that church all through the song. Finally, near the end, I got to my feet and walked the eight or ten feet to the altar. As I knelt there, Ross came over and put his hand on my shoulder: "Bless you, Doug, God bless you."

A year later, I went forward again at some meetings which featured Herb Thompson, a gospel singer and my childhood idol. He knew I liked to sing and often called me up to do a number.

During high school in Anderson, I think I wore out the center aisle carpet at Park Place. I was a seeker at almost every revival—but never quite found what I was looking for. I just couldn't live up to what I thought I should be—much less what I thought God expected of me. I was never able to trust Him to accept me just as I was.

Spiritually, Huntington brought no improvement in my life. I was still going through the motions. Sometimes, I didn't even do that. To avoid facing people and the work I was supposed to be doing, I'd read until late at night and then sleep until noon. After lunch, I'd make some calls, usually to the homes of friends, and then come home for dinner. I did a lot of time-killing in those days. Many afternoons, I'd drive out along the Ohio River and park. I didn't fish or boat or anything—I just sat. Occasionally, I would read the books or magazines I had brought along. At this point, I should say something about my reading habits.

The near disaster at High Point had really scared me. I decided I would be very careful in my contacts with other women at Huntington. Therefore, I made it a point not to practice female solos without other choir members present. I stopped making house calls to women in the church unless I knew that someone else was at home. I no longer volunteered to take any female choir members home from practice. But then I began to undermine all my resolutions by the kind of books I bought to read. It is amazing now to think that, as broke as we were, I'd pay good money for trashy reading material. Maybe that's another indication of just how sick I was. With such a diet for my mind and thoughts, I am sure had I stayed in Huntington much longer, I would have ended up in serious trouble once again. The Lord probably knew this, for somehow He mercifully helped me get out of there in time.

Laura and I drifted further and further apart in Huntington. While we were in High Point, we thought that her pregnancy was the problem. But after Paula was born and a normal recovery period had passed, something was still missing in our relationship. My rejection left her confused and upset, and it left me feeling morose and guilty. I saw Laura as the mother of my child but not really as my wife.

To pass the time, Laura took Paula through the garden in her stroller or sat with her in the gazebo. She also used her training as a beautician to fix the hair of friends. Showing an average-looking girl how to make the most of her assets always gave Laura a sense of accomplishment. She kept busy at Huntington giving free permanents and haircuts. I badgered her into teaching a Sunday School class. Laura had always been too shy to teach, but she finally consented to try. On her first day, the kids got out of hand, and she left the room in tears.

She cried a great deal that year. Often, I came home and saw her cheeks wet and her eyes red, but I didn't inquire for fear she would tell me. Our communication lines were down, and we were too young to know we needed a repairman.

Once, I remember finding Laura in the bedroom on her knees, praying. I overheard her asking God to help her be the kind of wife I wanted. I interrupted her to ask if I could have some lunch. She was startled, but got up from her knees, wiped her eyes and ran to the kitchen. I made some tearful prayers of my own, but most of the time I just moped. Everything was wrong with me—my job, the church, Laura—everything.

There were some light moments—church events, trips, nights with friends . . . We didn't have a television set, so we managed to get an invitation almost every Saturday night to watch wrestling or Sid Caesar and Imogene Coca. Milton Berle was also big about then. We often had friends in for pizza and a game of "Rook" or "Sorry." We also went skating with Bill and Jean Harbour. I take that back. *We* didn't go skating—*I* did. Laura usually stayed home with Paula. Incidentally, the Harbours surprised us one day by presenting us with a used TV. The young people of the church had bought it for us.

Other good friends there included Wink and Eleanor Patrick and Ray and Kathlene Sager. Ray, who ran a used auto parts business, was a guy I really liked, and we had many man-to-man talks. What a horse of a man he was! Once, a car fell off its jack and pinned him underneath. He called for help and held the car off his chest until someone came and jacked it up again. He walked away unscathed.

There were occasional warm family moments. I wasn't much of a Dad and seldom had anything to do with Paula. Once, I sneaked up on Laura while she was in the kitchen and took Paula, who was then about four months old, and sat her inside a galvanized pail. I opened the kitchen door and slid the pail toward Laura. She screamed until she saw the contents of the pail. All you could see was the top of Paula's head and her big, brown eyes peeking over the top of the bucket. We had a great laugh.

Most of the time, though, we were pretty unhappy, and

it was usually my fault. I browbeat Laura, criticized her cooking, her clothes, her housekeeping, her care of Paula. Anything and everything. I was inconsiderate of her in almost every way. I remember bringing home a group of fellows who had just gotten back from a successful fishing trip. I got Laura Lee out of bed at 2:00 A.M. to fry the fish. She should have hit me with the skillet!

On another occasion, Laura took Paula to her mother's in Nebraska for a couple of weeks. While she was away, I called at the home of one of the female members of the church one afternoon. Just as I was leaving, a member of the choir drove by. The woman in the car waved, but she had a rather surprised look on her face.

A few days later, Ivan called me in and suggested I had made some "errors in judgment."

"Are you suggesting I've been immoral?" I asked, heatedly.

"No, only that you have acted foolishly and ill-advisedly," Ivan answered, hoping to avoid a confrontation. "We will pay you for the full twelve months, but you are relieved of your duties and are free to look for another job. We went into this on a trial basis. Let's just say that we decided the church can't afford a full-time minister of music."

I had been there ten months. Another ringing success for Dale Oldham's son! I taunted myself all the way home. It was a weak attempt at humor. I was mad at the seeming injustice on one hand; frustrated and ashamed on the other that I couldn't get things better ordered in my life. Then, too, I'd have to call Dad, make up some kind of alibi for my departure, and, of course, ask him to help me find another job.

Laura and Paula came home in a few days. I told her that Ivan and I had had a misunderstanding and, by mutual agreement, had decided to call it quits. She didn't question me. Once again, the old pattern was repeated.

CHAPTER 7
A Running Man

The news that I was out of a job at Huntington came just before a scheduled month's leave of absence. Dad had bought a house trailer and had invited us to spend August with them at some camp meetings in Canada. I was looking forward to leading the music and singing. The month also gave us a little more time to find a new location.

Before we drove over to Anderson to meet my folks, I called Dad and told him I was leaving Huntington. I'm sure I put most of the blame on Ivan, though he certainly was not responsible in any way for my difficulties. He had been very patient and kind to me while we were working together. I'm sure, also, that I said I wanted out, not that I was being forced out.

Dad had talked recently with Herb Streeter, pastor of the Royal Oak Church of God, now Woodlawn, and knew he was looking for a minister of music. I called him and discovered that the position was still open. We set up an appointment for an interview in Detroit. A couple of days later, I drove up and was hired on the spot. Once again, I moved to a bigger, more prestigious church, and my salary doubled to $100 a week.

Before we moved to Michigan, we had the month of August

with Dad and Polly. Laura was elated at the prospects of the trip. So was Dad. "It'll be great to be together again—one big happy family," he said. It didn't quite work out that way.

For one thing, a trailer is mighty confining for one family. But when you put two families together, especially with a baby, it can become very trying. Paula was still not a year old, and her crying got on Polly's nerves. Laura was looking forward to attending the meetings. With the trailer close by, she figured she could put Paula to bed and that she would sleep through the services without any problem. The first night in beautiful Banff Park beside Lake Louise, Laura and I decided to take a moonlit walk after the service, leaving Paula asleep in Grandma's care. While we were gone, she fell out of her crib and woke up screaming. Polly did everything possible to quiet her and get her back to sleep. By the time we returned, she was nearly in tears herself. From then on, Polly felt that it would not be wise to leave the baby alone during the services. Since she was required to play the piano, Laura would have to stay behind and babysit.

Laura was disappointed and unhappy with the arrangement, but didn't say anything until near the end of the meeting. One day, as Laura and I were walking along the shore of the lake, a glacier cracked, sending an enormous boom echoing across the water. When the ear-shattering sound had subsided, Laura said, "That's exactly what I'd like to say to Polly!"

The time with Dad was good for me. It was the first extended period we had spent together since I began college. Something had changed in our relationship—for the better. I had been out on my own, and though I hadn't been very successful, Dad was proud of me because I was working in the church. Maybe he didn't know what a mess I was making of things, or he might have known more than I thought he did; but he refused to give up on me.

As a kid, I had always felt pressure when I was around him. I felt a constant need to prove myself. He did everything well, and I tried to measure myself by his performance. Of course, I didn't come off too well in these comparisons. Whenever I failed, I felt I'd let my folks down and was unworthy of them.

Hearing Dad preach was always an uplifting experience for me. In the meeting in Canada, he related many of the stories from his boyhood that illustrated God's concern and love. They were warm, personal stories like the one he tells about himself as a boy riding on a horse-drawn wagon with his grandfather in Oklahoma.

"We were going to Engels, the town nearest our home," he recalled. "The river had spilled its banks, and fording it would be a tricky job. This day, when we entered the swirling chocolate waters, swollen even more by a heavy rain, I crowded close to Grandpa. He urged the horses on, slapping the reins as the water rose around their middles, over their backs and up their necks, until only the animals' straining heads cleared the stream. The water rose inside the wagon, too. I had to raise my feet up on the dashboard to keep them from getting wet. I was growing more and more scared—maybe the current would carry us downstream, dash us against some rocks, upset us, drown us! Just as my anxiety reached the breaking point, I felt Grandpa's right arm grip my shoulders and pull me closer to him. All my fears and apprehension vanished in that instant."

"That was half a century ago," Dad continued. "But I've never forgotten the strength and reassurance I felt when Grandpa put his arm around me and quieted my pounding heart. That's what it's like when you let the Heavenly Father put His arm around you. Taken into His care, you're safe, protected, free from anxiety. And once you've been wrapped by those everlasting arms, you need never worry about anything again. He knows the treacherous waters and will take you across safely."

How I wanted to feel those arms about me! I knew about

the storms of passion and doubt; I'd been engulfed by floods
of guilt and failure, but, somehow, I had never been able
to feel those arms about me.

Dad and I had a good many talks during that month. Deep
talks. He knew that I was doing some searching, that I was
troubled and without peace, and he tried to help me. One
day, as we were out in the woods walking a narrow, winding
mountain trail, we came face to face with a huge bull moose.
We weren't ten feet apart. I was frightened and ready to run,
but Dad put his hand on my arm and anchored me to the
spot. Slowly, he raised the camera he had hanging from a
strap around his neck and snapped a picture. When the shutter
clicked, the moose turned and bounded off.

"Never run," Dad counseled, as he recocked the shutter,
"It never solves anything."

When we returned from Canada, we made the move to
Royal Oak. It was a positive step for us. Herb Streeter was
a dynamic preacher, and he and his wife, Gail, made a great
team. He was also an excellent counselor and must have sensed
the deep anxieties that gnawed on me. I don't suppose it was
hard to see, though I thought I had things well hidden. As
I look back, I'm sure I didn't fool many people. Herb offered
some real help. He was genuinely interested in me as a person,
and that interest was flattering and encouraging to me. While
my reaction to people who didn't seem awed by my talents
was usually that *they* were at fault, deep inside I was just
like everybody else. I wanted to be cared about.

Herb knew what I needed, and more than anyone else thus
far in my life, he gave me a sense of worth and accomplishment. He took me into his confidence and shared his personal
problems and goals. Most of all, he made the job I was doing
seem important. I had always been able to erect defenses
against others, but I couldn't resist Herb's concern and faith
in me. For the first time, I began to apply myself as a minister

of music. I had been a reluctant worker from the start because I had so many hangups about the ministry. I had always said being a minister was the last thing I wanted to do. Until I came to Detroit, I never enjoyed my work.

Now, I began to study music seriously. While in Huntington, I had audited a few music classes at Marshall College, but I really wasn't very serious about improving myself. At Royal Oak, it was different. I remember the impression one book made on my mind. It was Kettering's *Steps Toward a Singing Church.* From it, I learned such things as how to conduct auditions for children's choirs and their operation. I learned pointers on how to get maximum attendance and loyalty. I learned new rehearsal techniques and many sources for material and literature.

I began watching other choirs more closely, particularly the good ones. I wanted to know what made them good. If I heard something I liked—some arrangement, some special interpretation—I tried the technique on my choir. It was trial and error and I made a good many errors, but I began to learn.

I heard the Blackwood Brothers Quartet for the first time while I was in Detroit and was really impressed by their sound and technique. I "borrowed" several of their arrangements and adapted them to my use.

Herb was an advocate of Youth for Christ and was enthusiastic, experimental and precedent-breaking. One Valentine's Day, I remember his making an unusual Sunday morning entrance—through a big, red paper heart. His sermon was based on I Corinthians 13. On Christmas Sunday, he brought a birthday cake to the pulpit to remind everyone that we were celebrating the Lord's birthday. I had been raised in more conservative churches, and this was a new style for me. It was attention-getting and unique. Young people were quick to respond. It made a deep impression on me.

I was in charge of youth work, too, but I really wasn't good with kids. Herb's wife, Gail, was one of the best I've ever known. Although the responsibility fell on my shoulders, I'm sure that the real impact that was made in the Youth Department centered around her contributions.

My point of concentration was on music. One day, Herb showed me a brochure advertising a music workshop conducted by Fred Waring at Delaware Water Gap in Pennsylvania. "Sounds good to me," he said. "Would you be interested?"

I couldn't believe the church would send me there for a week, but it was only the first of four Waring training weeks I was to attend. These were great times of learning for me.

I'll never forget that first trip to Pennsylvania. The workshop was held at a summer camp that had been a boys' school. We stayed in barracks-type quarters, with beds and running water, but little else. The food was good, though, and the teaching superb.

At one of the first meetings, Fred turned to me and asked, "What do you do?"

"I am a singer," I replied.

"Are you a musician?"

"No, sir," I answered.

"Let me shake your hand," he said. "No singer is a musician, but few will admit it."

There were many things I learned from Fred that helped me both as a soloist and as a director.

"If people don't show up to hear you," he instructed, "reprimand yourself, not the people. They know what they like, and, if you aren't giving them something worth coming back for, you've failed."

He also had a maxim that all choir directors should memorize. It goes like this: A good choir director never has a bad choir for long, and a bad choir director never has a good choir for long.

Fred Waring's approach was simple and honest. His music and programs always reflected that sincerity and candor that

audiences all over the world have come to appreciate. He was
the first to impress on me the importance of visuals—costumes
and props, little touches that make such a difference. Fred
also used easy, natural movement that keeps an audience
interested, expectant. Some of the motions and gestures were
kids' stuff, I thought, when I first saw them. However, in Fred's
talented hands, they took on professional polish. He was a
hard worker, and he showed me that the difference between
adequate and excellent was only a few more minutes' work.

When I returned from the workshop, I put to work some
of the things I had learned. One of the first things I tried
with my choir was a John Peterson cantata. The night I gave
the books to the choir, I asked them for five hours of their
time—6:00 P.M. to 11:00 P.M.

The first hour, I played the recording of the cantata which
runs forty-eight minutes. "All I want you to do is listen," I
suggested. I cranked my Magnavox way up and bombarded
them with the music. The second hour, I passed out books
and told them to follow the music, but not to sing, hum or
do anything but study their parts. The third hour, I asked
the choir to sing with the music. I kept the Magnavox volume
high enough that it swallowed the choir. I wanted them to
absorb it. The fourth hour, I matched levels between the choir
and the recording. Finally, in the fifth hour, I turned the
recording off and ran through the cantata from cover to cover
except for solos. It worked beyond all expectations, and I have
frequently used the technique with equally good results.

Another trick Fred taught me was pre-teaching. This re-
quires advance work with maybe eight of the best choir voices.
After they have learned the music, the work is introduced
to the choir, and the members can then follow the pre-taught
leads. It is very valuable when time is limited.

During this time, I also began studying voice at the Detroit
Conservatory. Russ Skitch was my teacher. I had always
wanted to try opera. As a kid, I had listened to recorded operas

and admired such top tenors as Jusse Bjoerling and Jan Peerce. In the shower or off to myself, I often tried to imitate their style. However, it didn't take Russ Skitch long to dampen those ambitions.

"You don't have the range," he said. "Forget it. You have average range, however, and good quality." He told me that I had to make a decision: "You can either choose to be a tenor with a broad range or a baritone with a limited range." He encouraged the latter, and it proved to be the right choice.

His help was invaluable. Russ gave me some essential instruction without which I could not have progressed. I paid for one thirty-minute lesson a week—$10 I really couldn't afford. Russ gave me two or three others, free. He also allowed several of our sessions to run longer. We had an easy, warm relationship that made the lessons doubly useful.

I was singing solos at most every church service by now, but I was struggling. My personal conflict kept a lid on my voice, and I was not free in style or delivery. Of course, power and effectiveness were lacking because of these deficiencies. Still, I was beginning to develop as a singer and choir director. Gradually, my reputation began to spread and it was gratifying to me.

Spiritually, though, it was a stalemate. I was still faking hospital calls—trying to grab God with one hand and hold onto the world with the other.

Although I avoided situations with women that might prove a temptation, I found myself driving daily down Woodward Avenue past the smut shops. Sometimes, I could talk myself past several of the shops. But before I had passed through the "adult bookstore" district, I nearly always weakened and would spend half an hour browsing. I felt cheap and degraded, and resolved not to go again, but I did not have the spiritual strength to break with this sordid part of my life.

My problem did take on one new wrinkle. When the books and magazines no longer satisfied me, I turned to burlesque and, behind dark glasses, made many a foray to the Gaiety in Detroit. It's a wonder I never got caught. I might have been better off if I had. So the guilt continued to build.

Laura and I were not getting along any better, either. We went through the outer appearances of making a go of things, but our relationship was hollow and empty. We had less and less to share. Laura had gone to work in a beauty shop on the south edge of Birmingham, and I am sure this interest kept her from coming apart. Her employer was a warm, understanding man who gave her a sense of worth. She still had hopes of working things out and kept trying to resolve our differences. Her strong faith was all that kept things together. That—and Paula.

Paula was two by now, and she was about our only common interest. Though I didn't pay much attention to her, I loved her in my own limited way. When we were out in the car, she would stand on the seat next to me, her arm around my neck. Once, on a trip back to Anderson, I felt her head droop onto my shoulder. She had gone to sleep standing up.

One day, while visiting friends, we had quite a scare. Their beautiful golden cocker spaniel apparently became jealous of all the attention being given Paula, and he bit her in the face. The lady, a nurse who worked for a physician, had him put in the necessary stitches. Laura held Paula while the treatment was going on. I couldn't watch. Already, she had gotten her chubby little hands into my heartstrings, and I couldn't bear to see her hurt.

Speaking of dogs, we nearly always had a dog, and Detroit was no exception. Someone gave us a big collie that had been badly mistreated. He was a real mental case, but I agreed to give him a home. Maybe I identified with him. He was frightened by everything—running water, noisy kids, airplanes, and especially passing cars. He wouldn't venture outside unless I went with him, and, if a car passed by, he would run lickety-split back to me and leap into my arms. That must have been quite a sight—a fat man trying to keep his balance when that collie sailed into his arms. In the end, we had to give him up. It broke my heart to part with him—I actually broke down and cried when I left him with the original owners.

Though I could be tender with animals, I was less than kind to Laura. I was constantly undermining her, complaining, picking. But I hit a new low when I revealed something to her one night on a trip to Anderson.

We were somewhere near Angola, Indiana, north of Anderson. We had been talking seriously about our situation when I said something that caused Laura's mouth to drop open in utter disbelief. Though I was driving and it was nearly dark, I could see her face grow pale. It happened in an instant. Though I can't remember exactly what I said, her response was, "Then the rumors about you are true. You were seeing someone."

"Yes," I admitted. It was a devastating blow, but I imagine subconsciously I wanted to let Laura Lee know and really wipe her out. As soon as I told her, I knew I had made a mistake. She was deeply wounded and, like a scared puppy, began to quiver and cry. She kept her face turned away from me for the rest of the trip to my folks' house.

I couldn't think of anything to say, except, "I'm sorry."

Laura sobbed, "So am I, Doug. So am I."

CHAPTER 8

No Place To Stop

Bad news usually has company. Just as Laura was trying to adjust to my devastating news, she discovered that she was expecting again. The timing couldn't have been worse. Sick at heart and sick of body, she quit her job at the beauty shop—the most pleasant outlet she had—and, on doctor's orders, went to bed.

Before I admitted my guilt, Laura had feared that I was unfaithful, but, somehow, she had managed not to believe it. Her daily prayer was that I had not been involved with anyone in the past and that God would keep me out of trouble in the future. Now, with her confidence undermined, she was attacked with fresh doubts each day. I could do nothing to rebuild her faith in me. She distrusted me totally. Because she was so weak physically, the imaginings of her mind rambled wildly.

She feared now that our marriage could not be salvaged. Every time I left the house, there was some indication of her anxiety and distrust. She also developed a personal phobia that something terrible was going to happen to her. When I was away on trips—usually to evangelistic meetings between Monday and Friday—she would hire a girl from the church to stay all night with her. She was afraid to be alone. I tried to tell her she had nothing to be alarmed about. With the dog (we had replaced the collie with a black terrier-mutt), a fence around the house and locked doors, no one was likely to get in. But I could not reach her. One night, I came home and found her sitting in a chair, huddled against an inside wall, crying uncontrollably. I tried to console her, but she was near hysterics.

I really didn't know what to do. My feelings vacillated between pity and disgust. The fact that her insecurity might be driving her toward a breakdown didn't dawn on me. I was still so mixed up that I couldn't recognize or sympathize with someone else's needs.

Most of the time, I only added to her problems. Once she knew that I had been unfaithful, her jealousy took many forms. She was often critical, which was contrary to her nature. In retaliation, I found new ways of hurting her. Once, after suggesting she do a duet with me and after practicing with her for several weeks, I blew up when she got off-key. "You can't sing well enough to do this. Let's forget it!" That was not true. Laura had sung in college, had performed the lead in a musical and possessed a beautiful alto voice, but I wanted to say something mean, and I succeeded.

Only when she became ill during her second pregnancy, requiring a week's hospitalization, did I realize how sick she was. She was six months along when the doctor told us she was again in danger of losing the baby. He sent her to the hospital for a week. That incident shook me up. Physical illness is more tangible and this time I responded with genuine concern. When Laura came home, the doctor ordered her to bed until the baby came, so I was in charge of the house. With Polly's help and that of Laura's mother, who also came to lend a hand, we managed to get by.

By now, I was singing more and more and so was required to be away for several days each week. My solo work on the Christian Brotherhood Hour, as well as that with the quartet, gave me national exposure. Invitations to sing far and wide became more frequent. I enjoyed both the travel and the singing, but I also liked the money. Laura had made $150 or more each week at the beauty shop before she had to quit. As the church was paying me $100, and I could make $150 or more on the road during the week, our financial picture had brightened. I placed a high value on material things, and we spent every cent we made on something. Usually, it was something we didn't need, but I simply had to indulge my rich tastes.

After a year and a half in Detroit, my frequent absences from the church during the week became a problem. I was always present for my choir and music work on weekends, but I was omitting other obligations, such as hospital and home calls and the youth work. Finally, the official board set some limits. I was to take no more than two weeks off for special services, plus my annual vacation. I talked with Herb about this decision.

"This just isn't going to work," I told him one day in his study. "I have opportunities to sing every week."

"I know you do." Herb leaned back in his chair, his hands clasped behind his head. "But a minister must answer to his congregation and the boards which represent the members. You'll just have to toe the line, or else."

"Or else—what?" I pressed.

"Or else . . ." he paused, "find a new job that allows you more freedom." Herb smiled when he finished. He was not telling me what to do, just advising what he would do in my position. Herb's support during this period of my life was immeasurable. For once, a pastor wanted me to stay on—which was a switch. I knew that Herb believed I had a future in church music, and he wanted to encourage me.

"Thanks, Herb," I said. "That's the way I feel, too."

A few minutes later, I was talking with R. C. Caudill, pastor of the Middletown (Ohio) Church of God. R. C. had inquired about my availability a few weeks earlier during one of my singing engagements. I had told him at the time that I was happy in Detroit, but I would give his offer some thought.

R. C. was an old, fire-ball type of pastor who had built the Middletown church into the second or third largest in our denomination. Dad had sung for him before he himself went into the pulpit ministry, so R. C. was an old family friend. Dad was pleased when he heard that I was joining forces with him. The Middletown church agreed to pay me $135 a week, provide a parsonage and give me the freedom I needed to fill dates around the country.

When I told Herb I was moving to Middletown—the same day he had given me his indirect advice—he responded, "That's the trouble with you, Oldham, you're just too indecisive. You don't know how to make decisions."

Laura took the news with mixed emotions. She liked Detroit. It had been a relatively calm port for us compared to some of our other homes. And, of course, in her condition, she really wasn't strong enough to make another move.

"How will we ever manage?" she asked, "I can't do anything."

"You won't have to turn a hand," I assured her. "Polly, Dad and I will handle it."

"Oh, no," she frowned. I knew she preferred that my folks not be involved, but there was nothing she could do. In April, 1955, we moved to Middletown. I suggested that Laura travel by ambulance or train, but she wanted to go by car and got along fine.

Usually, moving into a new home in a new town is an exciting time. The people in the church are anxious to get acquainted, and there are always invitations to meals and parties. But Laura was in no condition to do any socializing. As she had with Paula, she spent most of her time in bed, miserably weak and sick.

A few weeks after we arrived, the women of the church planned a shower for her. She had hoped to attend for a little while. As it turned out, she didn't make it to the shower, and I was so distraught that I forgot to call the ladies to explain. I had other things on my mind. Earlier in the day, Laura had started hemorrhaging. We were so new in town I didn't even know how to get to the hospital. I had helped Laura into the car, started the motor and was ready to pull out of the drive before I realized that I didn't know where I was going. The lady who lived in the other side of our duplex gave me hurried directions.

When the doctor saw Laura, he rushed her into the operating room to prepare her for an emergency Caesarean section.

"Your wife is in critical condition," he said, "and the baby is in danger. We have no time to lose."

Outside the delivery room, I prayed as I had never prayed before. The thought of losing Laura shook me to the bone. I was ashamed of all I had said and done to her, and I wanted another chance. "I'll treat her differently, Lord," I promised.

An hour later, I learned that the baby had been born—a girl (to be named Karen LaRue)—but that there were still complications. Laura had lost a great deal of blood, and the operation had been a difficult one. The baby was having a hard time breathing and had not responded to the doctor's first attempts to get her to inhale. It was feared that she might have suffered brain damage.

"All we can do is wait and see," the doctor said. And I waited.

Occasionally, through the night, I received inconclusive reports: "They're doing as well as can be expected" . . . "resting comfortably" . . . "no change" . . .

It was a long, long night. I sat in the waiting room; I paced the hallways; I drank coffee in the cafeteria; I walked the sidewalks outside. There was plenty of time to think. All the nonsense in which I had been involved, the meaninglessness of my life, the brutality of my words and actions broke into my consciousness and shamed me mercilessly.

"Oh, God," I pleaded, "help me to find a way out. Please

don't take Laura away from me. Please give me another chance. Please make the baby well. Please don't leave me alone . . ."

The night dragged on. Sleep was snatched in fifteen-minute catnaps followed by more pacing or conversation with fellow sufferers who shared the little information they had been able to glean about their loved ones.

Finally, morning came and, with it, the news that Laura was making progress. She had gotten a good night's rest and was regaining her strength. Karen had cried during her night in the incubator. This was good news. Furthermore, the doctor's examination revealed that she was normal—premature and small, but generally healthy.

"Thank God," I kept saying to myself. Outside the hospital in the bright morning light, a new exhileration filled my tired body. Maybe things are going to turn around now, I thought. At least, I could hope.

Mrs. Makings came again to help and stayed for several weeks after Laura and the baby came home from the hospital. By the time she left, things had returned to normal for us.

A little while after Laura's mother left, one of the strangest things happened. To this day, I don't know how to explain it fully, but it was totally real to us that night.

Laura had had her hands full in Middletown with Paula and the new baby. Though Paula was now three years old and no particular problem, Karen was still an infant who needed constant attention. She would wake up about every two hours, needing to be fed. Because I didn't want to be disturbed, I often slept in a room at the other end of the house, down a long hallway. Laura's mental and physical strain was severe, and she could have used some help, but I didn't offer it. I think I changed one diaper all the time the girls were growing up. Early one morning, all her anxieties jelled.

About 2:00 A.M., Laura was awakened by something other

than Karen's familiar cry. She was certain someone else was in her room. Laura was terrified, frozen to her pillow with fear. There was a nightlight on, but she could see nothing. She could hear nothing. It was simply a feeling—the sensation that something or someone was there. When she was able to move, she sat up slowly and attempted to locate the Presence.

It seemed that it was near the door which led down the hall to my room. She wanted to scream but felt she didn't dare. She was afraid to try to burst through the door by the Presence to reach me, because, even if she succeeded, the Spirit which she now discerned to be evil, would be left alone with Karen. Suddenly, a new fear gripped her. Tiny Karen, whose strength had been less than robust from birth, was the target! The Presence was going to harm Karen! With that thought, Laura managed to leave the bed and run to Karen's crib, placing herself between the Spirit and the sleeping child.

Karen slept peacefully, unaware that her mother stood an arm's length away, shielding her from an unseen force. Laura stood there for a long time, trembling.

"Go away," she finally said in a voice capable of no more than a whisper. "In God's name, go away."

Surprisingly, she sensed that something moved away. A strange heaviness left the doorway.

"It's gone," she sighed.

"Picking up the baby, Laura moved toward the doorway. The sinister Presence was still out there somewhere, but she felt it was possibly on the stairs that ran beside the hallway. Taking a deep breath and doubling herself over Karen's body, she ran toward my room, screaming, "Doug, help me, help me!"

I awakened with a start, bolted up in bed and turned on the light.

"What in the world is wrong?" I asked.

Her face was ashen and her eyes were filled with tears. I pulled her close. Her skin was clammy and her hands were shaking like leaves in the wind. She told me the story.

"You've only had a nightmare," I reassured her.

"No," she said emphatically. "There is, or was, something out there."

I reasoned some more, but she would not budge from her story, and she would not go back to her room.

"Listen, Laura, I have a big day tomorrow. Please go to sleep and let me do the same. We'll talk about this bad dream in the morning." Still, she wouldn't move. The thought crossed my mind that she was cracking under the strain of the difficult birth and sleepless nights.

"Then, I'll walk you back to your room."

Putting on my slippers and robe, I stepped out into the hallway. I had yawned and shuffled about halfway to her room when I felt a strange sensation. Now, *my* heart skipped a beat. There was something up ahead—in the doorway of Laura's bedroom. It wasn't visible or audible, but there was definitely a . . . a Presence there!

"Stay where you are," I told Laura who was walking behind me.

"Who's there?" I challenged. There was no answer.

"Take my hand," I ordered. And, like a scene straight out of a Grade B science fiction thriller, Laura and I cautiously moved toward the doorway. At the entrance, we made a run for the bed. She continued to hold Karen.

"It was trying to hurt Karen, I'm sure," she whispered.

"Then hold her."

I put my arm around them and, for at least half an hour, we huddled together in fear, wondering if this Death figure would attack or retreat. Finally, I suggested we sing, and we began to sing all the old hymns we could think of. Then we prayed, imploring God to remove this Presence and save us. Finally, in desperation, I commanded: "In the name of Jesus Christ, leave us and never return!"

As we prayed, there was a sudden lifting of gloom and fear—something had left the doorway.

"It's gone," I told Laura.

"Yes, I know," she replied.

In that instant, we both felt an unbelievable peace and tranquility sweep over us. Our nightclothes were wet with perspiration, and we were exhausted from the ordeal, but we felt a joy and a reassurance that is indescribable.

"He really cares," Laura said, somewhat amazed. "He really cares." For her, saddled with an unstable husband, weak in body and anxious in mind, the experience offered a degree of reassurance which she needed as badly as I did. In retrospect, I didn't know what to make of the experience. In some ways, I thought it ominous, foreboding—a sign of worse to come.

The Middletown church was well organized and, for the first time, I had a large music program for which to plan. All my resources were taxed. In fact, I was in over my head. The church was accustomed to good music and knew the difference between good and mediocre, so I was forced to work harder than ever before. The music department had the largest budget I'd ever had to work with, so there were few excuses for not producing. The Board okayed an expensive renovation of the choir loft, and, when I complained about the piano, they authorized the purchase of a new one. I found that Jose Iturbi's nine-foot Steinway was for sale and arranged to buy it. What a grand sound that added!

We had a graded choir program, with a forty-member senior choir, a senior high girls' ensemble, a junior high choir and a children's cherub choir. The work was demanding, but rewarding. For me, this was another period of learning and development.

One of my best teachers in Middletown was Pop Tankersley, who was then about seventy years old. In his day, he had been a truly outstanding singer. Of course, age had taken some of the timbre from his voice and he sang a little wavery and off pitch, but he could move a crowd with his testimony and song. His real strength lay in the life he had led. Though my voice had youth and quality, I lacked Pop's emotional depth. Old Pop kept building me up. I needed his encouragement more than he knew. He talked with me about singing out of a full heart, but, most of all, he acted as if he believed in me and in a rich potential that I didn't even see myself. Though my actions didn't merit it, I wanted someone to believe in me.

Working with R. C. was much different than working with Herb in Detroit. Herb had supervised my work very closely. R. C. just showed me what had to be done and expected me to accomplish it. One Sunday morning, I entered the church office and found a note saying that R. C. had been called away to Kentucky very suddenly. The note closed with the words: "You take it all today." He meant for me to preach as well as handle the music. I nearly panicked for a moment. I knew I was not ready for anything like that, so I got someone else to bring the message that day.

There were many pleasantries associated with our two-year stay in Middletown. Though the church was larger than the one in Detroit, it was located in a smaller town where friendships were easier to form. During the last part of our ministry there, we lived less than a block from the church, and people were always dropping in after services. Ralph and Elaine Evans, Gene and Norma Hayes, Skeet and Ruthie Cruze, Clyde and Lois Tankersley and August and Marybelle Schmidt visited us often. The living room had a big, brick fireplace where we'd gather in the winter for popcorn, cokes and conversation.

But after the friends had gone home and Laura and I were left alone with each other, there wasn't much to talk about. By now, she was suspicious of every move I made and every woman I knew.

As in Detroit, I found that I was more satisfied with myself if I kept busy. There was lots of work to be done, and I plunged into it. I still had some misgivings about working as a minister of music in a local church, but I had made the decision to try. However, after a few months when the "new" wore off, I was still plagued by the inward thoughts and doubts that I had always had.

During Laura's close call with death when Karen was born, I had made a lot of promises to the Lord. He had certainly answered my prayers, and I was genuinely attempting to fulfill my vows to Him. But I was trying to imitate "His life in me." I made the right moves and said the right things, but I just didn't have Him abiding in me.

Because of those promises, I was very careful in my conduct with women in the church. Only once did I come close to slipping into my old pattern, and that was not altogether my fault.

Late one evening, as I was leaving the church, I heard a knock on the sanctuary door. Everyone else had left, the church was dark, and I was alone. When I opened the door, I found a female church member who lived in a nearby town. She wanted to talk with me about some problems she was having with her husband. We had talked only a few minutes when I realized what a dangerous situation was developing, and I left the church hurriedly.

As it turned out, some neighbors had seen her park her car and enter the darkened building. Concerned, they had called the pastor. He, in turn, had called my house.

"Tell Doug to go down and check things out," R. C. had told Laura.

"But he's at the church."

"Oh," he said, "I'll call him there." He tried but got no answer.

When I got home, Laura told me the story.

"That's strange," I countered. "When I was locking up, I heard something, but I looked all around and didn't find anything. I wonder what it was?"

I was to hear about this again very soon. Also about the

same time another situation developed that was to cause me trouble first at home and then at the church.

I remember Laura was particularly upset when she learned that I was taking several women from the choir to Anderson to try out for the Christian Brotherhood Hour Choralaires.

"Aren't there any men whose voices are good enough to try out?" she asked.

"Yes, but they can't get off work." It was true, but Laura was still uneasy. I found her intimations hard to accept as I was taking five women in the morning and coming home in the same day. It was hardly an opportunity to become involved!

We went ahead with our plans for the trip over Laura's objections. One of the women succeeded in making the radio choir. I was quite proud, but my pride was short-lived. A week later, R. C. reported that one of the women who failed in the auditions was upset.

"She complained to a member of the official board," he warned me, "and he's on my back. She claims you built her hopes up unnecessarily, and the board member feels you showed poor judgment."

"That just isn't so," I objected, wondering which of the other four girls had been affronted.

"Well, you can expect it to come up at the next board meeting," R. C. continued. "They want to talk with you about the matter. Incidentally, Doug, I've been meaning to ask you about another incident of several weeks ago. The neighbors called me and said a black Olds parked outside the church one night and a woman went inside. The church was dark, they told me. A short time later, you came out, then the woman. Do you know anything about it?"

I stared at him noncommittally, reluctant to answer. What's the use? I didn't even want to try to explain. Who'd believe me? I just shook my head and walked away.

CHAPTER 9

Fame And Fortune With Fred Waring

"Time to move along."

"An offer we couldn't turn down."

"We feel the Lord is leading."

"It's a challenging opportunity."

As often as we had moved, we knew plenty of things to say at a Farewell Service. We left without any fuss or scandal. No one wanted to bring out embarrassing accusations, so I was allowed to move on quietly.

Maybe this ability to move so quickly helped. R. C. had talked with me on Thursday; I had made arrangements to go to Ashland on Friday; we moved on Sunday night. Most folk probably believed us, but there must have been a string of people from Hanover to High Point who shook their heads knowingly each time I transferred.

I knew Laura would be unhappy when she learned we were moving to Ashland, Kentucky. After all, Kentucky was in the South where she had had two bad scenes—in High Point and Huntington. The memory of those experiences was still too vivid and the hurts too deep to welcome an encore. A good many of our Middletown friends were from the "Promised Land"—Caanan-tucky. But Laura Lee didn't anticipate life there as flowing with milk and honey! Her eyes watered when

I broke the news to her, but she didn't cry. She knew that it wouldn't do any good. I had made a new deal and, as usual, had not bothered to consult her.

Ashland was only fifteen miles from Huntington, West Virginia, so it was really coming full circle for us. It had been five years since we had lived on beautiful Dunfee Hill in Huntington, and things had not improved much between Laura Lee and me. Huntington had marked the beginning of our estrangement as far as she was concerned. Paula had been just a baby when our relationship had begun to deteriorate in Huntington. Now, five years later, we had made little progress in solving the differences between us. We were both still young and really had little insight into what our problems were.

It seemed that I was beginning to be an accumulation of hangups. Some of them dated back to childhood and were just beginning to catch up with me. The head infections that I first had as a kid became more severe. Splitting headaches caused me to spend as much as two weeks at a time in bed. Though I never tried to analyze their cause, I was aware that I became particularly vulnerable to illness at Christmas and Easter when special music programs were scheduled and pressure on me was at a peak.

These head infections affected my throat and voice. Once, in Huntington, I became so concerned about the hoarseness that I went to a throat specialist. He advised me to quit singing for a year.

"Your throat tissues are damaged and need a rest, time to repair themselves."

"I can't quit," I protested. "I make my living with my voice."

"Suit yourself," he continued. "I can give you some medicine that may help, but if you don't take some time off, you may not be able to sing six months from now."

This jolted me quite a bit, so I did try to limit the use of my voice for a while. I also did a lot of foxhole praying: "God,

I can't be of any use to You as a singer unless You do something about my voice." Slowly, it improved.

Another problem that became an overpowering burden at Ashland was my overweight condition. As a kid I had been average size—maybe a little underweight—until my eleventh birthday. Then I had my tonsils out and gained sixty pounds in one year. I must have weighed 180 pounds. Though I was dumpy, roly-poly, chubby—call it what you will—my weight didn't bother me much. I was fairly popular, and, though I probably would have preferred to be thinner, I accepted myself pretty much as I was. Once in a while, I can recall a guy razzing me about being fat, but I usually tossed such gibes off easily.

However, with all my other problems ganging up on me, by the time I reached Ashland, I had become something of a compulsive eater and oversleeper. Sleeping late was a good method whereby I could avoid facing myself any sooner than necessary. Often, I'd sleep in until noon. Laura didn't ride me about either problem. In fact, she knew that she could please me with her good cooking; and if I was asleep, I wasn't complaining. By now, everything was wrong. I complained endlessly. Every time I looked in the mirror and saw the fat blob reflected in it, I became more irate and found something or someone else to abuse verbally.

In his book *Games People Play*, Eric Berne has labeled one of the games "Look What You Made Me Do . . ." I blamed Laura for everything—and indirectly, I suppose, considered my weight problem her fault. I was up to 235 pounds by now, which is just plain fat when you hang it on a five-foot-nine-inch frame. I'd tried dieting several times with temporary success. After a month of stringent calorie-counting, I might be able to lose twenty pounds, and then gain it all back in a week of unrestrained gorging.

All that weight was making me lethargic. To keep going, I took massive doses of dexedrine. Before getting out of bed in the morning, I was taking fifteen grains and seven and one-half more after breakfast. If I had an important meeting or engagement in the evening, I needed fifteen more grains in the afternoon. Though I wouldn't have admitted it at the time, I was addicted to dexedrine, which is a stimulant, an "upper." Many kids use this drug for "kicks." I was no kid.

I got the dexedrine with a doctor's prescription. In every town, I made it a point to be on good terms with a druggist, usually a member of the church. Later, I took dexemill, an amphetamine, which is a delayed capsule that fires all day. I also took excessive doses of thyroid for energy.

I remember Dad took me aside one time and talked to me about my weight. He suggested I could do something about it, and should. I suppose it embarrassed him to have a son in my condition share the platform with him. I didn't take kindly to his counsel.

My woes multiplied. In addition to the marital problems, my reading habits, my obesity, my head infections, my threatened vocal cords and all my guilt about my shortcomings—I was developing a serious drug habit. I simply had no control, no discipline over my mind or body.

I did continue to petition God for help. I realized the wrong I was doing to myself and others, and I knew God alone was the source of help. Yet, I couldn't or wouldn't let go of my indulgences. Somewhere, deep inside, a small candle glimmered. Maybe that's the difference between growing up in a Christian and a non-Christian home. Then, Polly and Dad were praying for me. They never stopped believing that I would find myself—which is a testimony to their great faith. Whatever the reasons, I still had hope.

My work at Ashland could best be characterized with one word: interruptions. Though the minister, Willard Wilcox, was a spellbinding speaker and a warm, effective communicator, I wasn't around long enough to be of much value to him.

Willard had been in Middletown when I was called there,

and he moved on to Ashland ahead of me. He had served Yankee Road Church of God while I was at Crawford Street. I became acquainted with him through his radio ministry and frequently sang on his program which was aired over WPFB. Our friendship blossomed, and I looked forward to serving with him in Ashland. The brief time we spent together was enjoyable. Many ministers have Monday morning planning sessions with their staffs. Willard and I usually held our meeting on the local golf course or riding J. Harmon's horses over the mountains.

When we first started playing golf, I was able to clean him regularly. He hadn't played all that much. But Willard was a methodical guy who always does things right, and he wasn't satisfied for long with 110's. Soon, he was pressing me hard. It's a good thing I left when I did, because he was beginning to beat me regularly.

I liked Willard a lot and was impressed with his dedication and intelligence. Out of the hills of Eastern Kentucky along Big Sandy Creek, Willard was a rare combination. He had a fine education, but he didn't let it get in the way of his work. The result was that he was loved by almost everybody. I inherited a fine choir with some really good voices. The Barker family, well known in that area as singers, were members of the church and added their talented voices to the choir. I loved to go to the Barkers' place for an evening of relaxation. They were a jolly family, and we had some happy times together.

But by now, I was out of town as much as in. As my reputation as a soloist grew, I was invited more often to accompany Dad to special meetings throughout the country. I would handle the music—the hymn selections, the choir direction and the solos—and Dad would do the preaching. We had some outstanding meetings in terms of crowds and numbers of people saved.

I remember the excitement of such city-wide meetings as

those we conducted in Flint, Michigan; Princeton and Blue-field, West Virginia; Montesano, Washington.

The meeting at Montesano was typical of the way in which the attendance and interest grew. On the first night, we didn't have enough singers to form a choir. On the second night, there were twenty people. This was a disappointment, because I needed a large choir to do justice to the music we were using. By the third night, there were sixty voices; and, before we closed the meeting, over one hundred. The attendance increased from a couple of hundred to over a thousand. We held those meetings in a huge airport hangar. By our final night, you couldn't have found room for a Piper Cub if you had stood it on its nose.

People never sing well in dark, unattractive settings, so to add color, Polly and I cut crepe paper into long strips and draped them over wooden beams some twenty feet above the floor. This helped liven the drab appearance of the place. I spent the whole afternoon climbing in and out of those rafters, tacking streamers. At that time I must have weighed 280 pounds. So I wasn't too surprised when my friend, Al Blankenship, walked in and remarked: "This is the first time they've ever docked the Goodyear blimp in one of these hangars!"

Another funny thing happened during the meeting. Toward the end of the meeting, a mishap occurred in the choir. We had built temporary risers and imported church pews for seats. The last row in the choir was approximately six feet from the ground.

About halfway through the service, the choir did the special number we had rehearsed. At the conclusion, I motioned for the choir to be seated and turned to give the congregation the number of the next hymn. Suddenly, I heard the crowd gasp and sensed that their attention had shifted to something that was going on behind me. Out of the corner of my eye, I saw what had distracted them. The soles of fourteen shoes belonging to my basses sitting on the back row were lined up across the platform. In half a second, they followed their owners over the back of the stage to the floor. When the fellows had taken their seats, the pew, which we had forgotten to anchor, tipped and sent them over backward.

Now it was my turn to gasp. There was a thud when the seven men landed. I expected the worst. Certainly, someone must have been seriously injured. But there was no outcry, just a deafening silence. For at least half a minute, everyone waited and wondered. The first evidence of life was the mysterious reappearance of the pew. It rose from nowhere and was repositioned by some unseen force. Seconds later, in filed seven, red-faced basses. Nothing had been hurt but their pride.

My training with Fred Waring helped immensely during these meetings. Within a few minutes, I was able to take the voices of strangers who had never performed together and mold them into a singing unit. With a few behind-the-back directional signals, I could do on-the-spot arrangements that suggested much more rehearsal and practice than was often the case. With a sign, I could take the choir from a hum to an "oh" to an "ah" to lyrics, changing at the phrase line.

With a song such as "How Great Thou Art," it is possible to produce all kinds of powerful effects this way. We were also able to use this technique well at invitation time. I developed several notebooks, categorized and cross-referenced. I listed everything by keys, so a pianist or organist could follow me easily. People marveled at the ability of the instrumentalist to follow me, and though it did require that a person stay on his toes, the notebooks told the person at the keyboard exactly what to do. All he had to do was turn the pages. In a word, I guess you could say I was coming of age professionally.

Technically, I was singing as well as ever. Yet, I knew how shallow my spiritual impact was and depended on Dad or whomever was preaching to do the soul-winning. My singing and choir-directing were crowd-pleasing, flashy and colorful, but I wasn't much of an instrument for God—and I knew why.

During this time, I sang often with the Christian Brothers

quartet. Ron Patty was our tenor; Paul Clausen was baritone (until Paul Hart replaced him); Ernie Gross was bass, and I sang second tenor or lead. Carolyn Patty accompanied us. We recorded for Capitol as well as the Christian Brotherhood Hour. We were received warmly wherever we went.

Shortly after Laura and I moved to Ashland, I turned to the guys in the quartet. I had been advised that Fred Waring was planning a TV workshop in Pennsylvania that summer, and I wanted to go.

"We've come along fine in radio," I told Ron Patty, "but TV is the coming medium, and I think Fred could help us." Ron liked the idea fine as did Ernie and Paul, and we registered for the summer workshop.

In June, just a few weeks after we had moved into our house in Ashland, I left for Delaware Water Gap with the quartet for my fourth Waring workshop. It was a tremendous learning experience. However, we weren't prepared for what happened.

I was talking to Jack Best, Fred's rehearsal conductor, telling him about our quartet, when he said suddenly: "When are you going to let me hear you?"

"You mean you'd like to hear us?"

"Sure, maybe we could use you. Let's get together tomorrow afternoon about four."

Flabbergasted, I went back to our quarters to tell the boys. They couldn't believe that Jack might be interested. We were all excited. We rehearsed for several hours that night and the next day auditioned for Jack Best. Impressed, he told Fred about us. Before we knew it, the founder of the famous chorale was out in front, listening. We did several numbers, but the one that Fred liked best was "I Bowed On My Knees and Cried Holy." He had grown up in a conservative Methodist family, and the lyrics of that song moved him to tears. It is a beautiful old song:

> *I dreamed I went to a city called Glory*
> *so bright and fair.*

When I entered the gates, I cried Holy
  and the angels all met me there.
They carried me from mansion to mansion
  and, oh, the sights I saw.
But I said I want to see Jesus
  the One who died for all.
Then I bowed on my knees and cried Holy
  Holy, Holy;
I clapped my hands and sang Glory,
  Glory, Glory,
Glory to the Son of God.

When we had finished, Fred came up front and asked, "Would you like to come with us?"

We couldn't believe our ears, but we didn't answer immediately.

"Give us some time to think it over," Ron said, and we went back to our rooms.

"I think we should pray about it," Ron's wife suggested.

My response was yes, but not in answer to prayer. I just liked the idea. Two of the other three said they felt it was something God would have them do. However, Ron could not make up his mind. He had some personal reservations about identifying with a secular group—even a group as fine as Fred Waring's. One disappointment was that Ron's wife, our pianist, was not included in the offer. Fred had Mark Lowery at the organ to play for us.

When the workshop came to an end, Ron was still undecided, so we left without giving Fred an answer. There were two weeks before rehearsals began for the fall tour, so we had a little time. Finally, at the midnight hour, Ron decided it was right and called Fred to "count us in." A few days later, we were on our way back East to begin a new adventure.

Meanwhile, Laura had moved back to Anderson. She didn't like the house we had bought, and she knew practically no one in Ashland. While I was traveling with Fred Waring, she

decided that she would stay in Anderson. It was a risky financial situation. Taking leave from Ashland meant that I had
no salary coming in, and one thing we had forgotten to discuss
with Fred in our excitement was money. We were so busy
trying to ascertain God's will in the matter that we just assumed
the pay would be more than adequate. Actually, for the four
weeks of rehearsal, we weren't paid anything. Then, we recorded an album for Capitol in New York, and I received
my first check. Fred agreed to pay $150 a week plus lodging.
That left food and other incidentals which mount up quickly
on the road, so it was hardly a get-rich-quick job.

Dad and Polly offered Laura and the kids the efficiency
apartment they had built for Grandpa and Grandma Brown.
I suggested that we try to sell the Ashland house, but that
proved difficult when it was discovered that fresh-water springs
in the basement were threatening the foundation. Our whole
investment was in jeopardy. But I was sure my career had
taken the turn for which I had been hoping. Soon I'd be in
the chips—the name Doug Oldham would be a household
word!

I still wanted to serve the Lord with my voice, but not
through church work. From the beginning, I knew I had to
get away from that oppressive spiritual umbrella. The truth
was that I felt more guilt in the presence of committed Christians, and I thought I could escape these feelings by leaving
the scene. So I "ran away" with Fred Waring. It would have
been an escape from the church syndrome if it hadn't been
for the other guys in the quartet—all dedicated to the Lord's
will. Of course, I never hinted to them that I was out of it,
unconnected. When they prayed, I prayed. When they objected
to some risque material in the show, I objected. Eventually,
when Fred signed to do the Club Oasis TV Show (ciga-
rette-sponsored), I joined the boys in resigning because we
couldn't be associated with a product such as cigarettes. When
I think of the life I was living, it is hard to imagine I could

have condemned anyone for smoking, but I agreed with the others that we should quit—probably because I didn't think I could convince them to stay anyway.

The highlight of the fall was singing before Queen Elizabeth II and Prince Phillip. The Queen was visiting in the United States, and President Eisenhower invited Fred to bring his performers to the White House to entertain. It was a heady experience, shaking hands with a Queen and a President. We were incensed because the quartet, called *The Glory Voices,* didn't get to sing that night. But we did sing with the Glee Club.

Jeanne Steel, Gordon Goodman, Len Kranendonk, Eleanor Forgione, Frank Davis, Nancy Reep, Patty Beems and Poley McClintock were the headliners then, but we got our chance to do three numbers a night, and it was great experience. It gave me confidence which I needed so desperately.

We traveled that fall doing one-nighters from New York to Seattle; Los Angeles to Miami. A Greyhound Sceni-cruiser was our wheels. Fred didn't like to fly, and only when the situation demanded, such as our trip to Washington to perform before the Queen, would he agree to travel by plane.

The tour with Fred was exciting at first, but it was hard work. Traveling by bus overnight can wear you down. To pass the time, I read a great deal and slept. Whenever we had a rest stop, I walked and jogged to get some exercise. Once, I got more than I bargained for. The bus broke down out West, and, while we were waiting for repairs, John Borneman and I began hoofing it.

"Pick us up," we called back as we set out. Three hours later, we were still walking—hot, exhausted and foot-weary. Before we reached the next town, the bus caught up with us.

"The next time the bus breaks down, I'm going to sleep," I told John. He was too busy massaging his feet to answer.

I saw Laura twice during that fall season—once coming home overnight and once when we were booked in Columbus. Both occasions were wipe-outs. We simply had nothing to say to each other. The feelings of love I'd once had for her were dead. I imagine she was feeling the same way. But we were married, and, as Christians, we had to go on. So we went through the motions. Why we didn't call things off then can only be explained by the fact that divorce seemed out of the question with our religious background. Once again, the very things I was struggling against were working to keep us from ruining our lives completely at that point.

The last week of December, I returned to Anderson, proud of my association with Fred Waring. Our parting had been amicable. Fred understood, though he told us he felt we were making a mistake. Of course, my Christian friends congratulated me for making such a courageous stand and making the "tough" decision.

Now, I figured I had some credentials that would help me to find a career in singing apart from church music. Foolishly, I felt that people would be standing in line for my services. I stopped in Anderson long enough to get my clothes washed and pressed; then, I kissed Laura, Paula and Karen goodbye and headed to Chicago. The thought of descending from the cloud I was riding was the last thing I wanted to do. This dream may have been unrealistic, but it suited me fine.

I had done some recording for Christian Brotherhood Hour at the Universal Studio on Rush Avenue and had several good friends there. One of them was Bernie Clapper, who gave me a job in the recording studio's tape library. I loved it. I worked from 6:00 A.M. until 4:00 P.M. each day, editing tapes without any hassle or supervision. This exposed me to people in the recording industry, and I figured it would be only a matter of time until I got my next break. I sent money home to Laura along with brief notes. Our financial picture wasn't very bright, but we were surviving. Laura had gone back to work at Mary's Beauty Shop, but the money was not good, and she wanted to be home with the kids.

I was enjoying hobnobbing with casting directors, producers, arrangers, musicians and living the life of a bachelor. For some reason, I felt a peace. The pressure to be something I wasn't was gone. I could relax.

However, I was serious about one thing—my career. But it didn't take off as I expected. Night after night, I'd go back to my hotel room on North State Street. It was anything but plush—someone had covered the windows with paper and sprayed everything, including bed, chair, and floor, a sickly green. I would read the paper, listen to the radio, smoke a cigar (I had left the Fred Waring Show because of a cigarette sponsor) and go to bed. The next day, I'd make more calls, drop in on casting directors, audition—and wait.

About the only success was my radio soap commercial. I met Bernie coming out of Studio D one day. He had a frown on his face.

"What's the problem?" I asked.

"We've gone through about fifty singers trying to find somebody to satisfy Foote, Cone and Belding. Nobody's right."

I knew that Foote, Cone and Belding was the agency that handled the Dial soap jingles, so I asked Bernie if he thought I should go in and try out.

"Why not?" he muttered. "And take the janitor, too."

To make a long story short, in a month, all America was hearing my voice, singing:

> *For soap that gets you extra clean,*
> *It's Dial, Dial, Dial!*
> *For soap that keeps you extra clean,*
> *It's Dial, Dial, Dial!*

With residuals, I eventually earned $2800 for those twenty-two words. When Bernie heard the tape, he roared, "Oldham, you've got the original bathtub voice!" Just what I needed to break into the pop music field!

Finally, after a long, cold Chicago winter, I grew discouraged. On one trip home to Anderson, I learned that North

Side Church of God in Indianapolis was looking for a minister of music. My grandfather, William H. Oldham, had served the church as pastor in the 1920's, so there were nostalgic reasons for taking the assignment. Going back to church music was not something I wanted to do, but it was a job and I sure wasn't doing any good in Chicago. In the spring of 1958, I accepted the Indianapolis offer and prepared to move. We had finally sold our house in Ashland, though we lost badly on the deal.

Interestingly, after being turned down for six months, when I returned to Chicago to pick up my belongings and close out things at Universal, I found three "call backs" from casting directors. I had already packed my bags and said my goodbyes. The car was gassed and ready to roll. It was strangely ironic. Should I check them out? One of the phone numbers might be the key to the future. I toyed with the slips of paper for several seconds. Then, I wadded them up, aimed for the wastebasket and hit the road.

I've often wondered what would have happened if I had made those calls. I might still be running.

CHAPTER 10
Further Failures

So we were moving again. Unlike our moves in the past, we had no illusions that anything would be different in Indianapolis. We had been married almost eight years by now, and we both knew that a new setting probably wouldn't make any difference in the pattern of our lives. For one thing, the separation from Laura and the kids and from the pressure of church work had been surprisingly pleasant for me. I was going back to church music, but it was mainly to earn a living. I was not really excited about the prospects.

Laura went because it must have seemed to her the only thing she could do. She was desperately trying to find some way out of the cycle of failure and misery our marriage had become. She read everything that could possibly give any spiritual or psychological guidance as to why we weren't getting along. She was closer than either of us knew to finding a way out of the marriage without losing her soul. There had to be a way to make our home a haven of love where the girls could be raised as they should. I doubt that many women could have endured the mental anguish and unhappiness I caused Laura. But she clung tenaciously to her faith and managed, with God's help, to maintain some semblance of family order and stability.

I suppose the children, more than anything else, gave her reason for living. Paula was six when we moved to Indianapolis and Karen, three. Inside a year and a half, they had another sister, Rebecca, or Dee Dee, as she came to be known. Unlike Karen, Dee Dee was a full-term, robust, healthy child from the start.

Laura Lee busied herself with the kids, and we were able to put on enough front to have some social life with the members and friends in the church. While we were there, I served on the planning committee for a Billy Graham Crusade, working closely with a great guy, Bob French. He was the advance man for the Crusade. His Scottish-born wife, Joyce, and Laura became good friends, and we all had some wonderful times together.

One of our favorite after-work activities was to take a picnic out to Giest Reservoir. The French children, Paul and Steve, and our girls enjoyed playing together. Joyce and Laura fixed some great gourmet picnics, and we spent many hours together, talking and eating by lantern light.

At home, however, I was the same old Doug, making life miserable for everyone, including myself. Even the children had my number. As I pulled into the driveway one afternoon, I overheard a remark by Paula that hit me pretty hard. As soon as I got out of the car, I began to scold the girls about something they had left in my way. Meekly, they moved away, but Paula whispered to her sister, "We better go downstairs. He's mean again."

It hadn't taken long for me to feel the pressures of the church music harness. Once again, I began to relive the guilt of laziness, of avoiding what I was being paid to do, of the inability to control my appetite and of my shabby, materialistic, inner life. It was bad enough to see myself as I really was. But, when I had to pretend, in front of the entire church, that I was someone altogether different, the agony and conviction were almost more than I could bear.

But I was so vain and egotistical that I worked very hard to make sure I went over well. I selected songs that displayed the bigness and richness of my voice and showed my control over it. I was always nervous and tense before the Sunday morning services, and anyone who got in the way of "Dad's big moment" was subject to my wrath. Funny how one can be so unkind to his family and then expect to sing, convincingly, about God's care and compassion.

Each Sunday morning, Laura would work feverishly to get the family ready for church while I read the paper. I don't remember ever offering to help, and no matter how hard-pressed for time, Laura knew that asking would only have caused a scene.

Once in the car, I demanded total silence, wanting to compose myself for my "performance" ahead. The tiniest distraction or noise would send me into a rage. "Don't bother Daddy now," Laura would caution the children. But it has never been possible to keep our girls from talking and wiggling. To make matters worse, Polly and Dad had bought the girls new coats of plastic that looked like leather. On cold mornings, in particular, the plastic would crackle every time they moved, and I would shout, "Will you keep the kids still or throw those fool coats away!"

Our first home in Indianapolis was a lovely duplex in a nice neighborhood on Washington Boulevard. The church, North Side Church of God, later renamed Glendale, was about three miles away.

Joe Gilliam served as pastor. He and his wife, Marilyn, were very kind to us and had great rapport with the girls. Karen, who was three at the time, adored Joe. Whenever she saw him, she would call, "Here me am, Joe," and run headlong into his arms.

Joe was a sharp guy—young, lean, muscular and handsome with a sprig of wavy, chestnut hair usually punctuating his forehead. He was also a good preacher—smart and well organized. A few years later, he was an ideal choice for the presidency of Warner Pacific College and did a tremendous job in pulling the school out of a slump.

In the administration of his pastoral duties, Joe was very careful to maintain an aura of decorum. He suggested to me often that I should exercise greater care in my conduct with members of the church, especially the ladies. I was constantly creating problems for him.

I was very strict about attendance at the Wednesday night choir rehearsals. If a choir member missed rehearsal, he was not allowed to sing in the choir on Sunday. This policy led me into some heated arguments. But criticism really mounted when I excused one attractive, young lady and permitted her to sing after missing choir rehearsal. Naturally, Joe was on the spot and had to defend my actions.

Once, on a trip to northern Indiana, I confided to him that Laura Lee and I were having difficulties and that they were often a result of past indiscretions on my part. I don't remember going into much detail, and I thought we were good enough friends that I could share some things with him. He seemed understanding, asked some questions, made some sympathetic comments along the line that "true love never runs smooth," and that was it.

Later, I began to feel that our long conversation, coupled with my immature actions, gave him deep misgivings about my position as minister of music. From that time forward, there seemed to be a barrier between us. Joe wasn't ready to dismiss me, and I wasn't really looking for another job. However, after a year and a half, both of us would have welcomed a way to terminate my employment by the church.

The way out was just around the corner for me. It was about this time that I met Billy Zeoli, who was heading Youth for Christ in Indianapolis. I liked him right away. He was young, sharp, aggressive and very popular with kids. Billy invited me to sing at several of the Youth for Christ rallies. One day he said, "I want Warren Walker to hear you sing."

Warren Walker was the radio minister for the famous Cadle Tabernacle, the oldest continuous radio ministry in the country.

"Why?" I asked Billy.

"He needs a soloist, and I think you might be just the man he is looking for. I have prayed about it and the Lord said yes. I've already talked to Warren and now I'm asking you."

"Well, I'll give it a whirl."

A date was set up for me to sing at a Youth for Christ meeting, and Warren and Helen Walker came. That night I remember singing "Follow Me:"

> *I traveled down a lonely road*
> *And no one seemed to care,*
> *The burden on my weary back*
> *Had bowed me to despair,*
> *I oft complained to Jesus*
> *How folks were treating me,*
> *And then I heard Him say so tenderly, . . . "Follow*
> * me."*

Warren liked what he heard and asked if I was happy at North Side.

"Yes and no," I answered.

"Well, we might be able to find a place for you on the broadcast."

"Fine," I said, noncommittally. I felt that he wanted me, but I did not want to appear too eager for the job. I thought it would be better to wait for a definite invitation.

"Call me if you're interested."

"Okay," I called as I left with Billy Zeoli.

"You're in!" Billy was enthusiastic as we headed for the car.

"Think so?"

"Sure. He likes you."

I determined not to call Warren, and it was a week before he contacted me. "We can pay you $150.00 a week."

"You've got yourself a new singer," I said. A week later, I made my first appearance on the program.

Warren Walker was unlike anyone I'd ever come across in the ministry. He had married Helen Cadle, daughter of E. Howard Cadle who founded the Cadle Tabernacle. Warren came to the Tabernacle in 1955 when the program was sagging and soon pumped new life into the operation. Under his direction, the Tabernacle soon had a mailing list of 150,000 names instead of 60,000; the monthly magazine took on a new life and was increased from four pages to thirty-two. The program was carried daily over 50,000 watt WLW out of Cincinnati, as well as on thirty-five other stations across the country. Five TV stations included it in their programming. Warren was a charismatic figure. I was thoroughly impressed. He was a stylish dresser and moved in influential circles in Indianapolis. He believed that God wanted his ambassadors to go first class.

"You've got to think big, Doug," he would say. Thinking big easily became my working philosophy.

The *Wall Street Journal, Fortune* Magazine, Napoleon Hill's books and the McGraw-Hill business success series became regular reading matter. Warren got me a membership in the Indianapolis Athletic Club, bought the family a lifetime membership in the National Health Studio and put me on a physical fitness program—exercise and diet. I didn't lose any weight, but I did shift it around. How I disliked going to the steam room, working out with weights and exercise machines! The only thing I looked forward to was the massage and shower.

Meanwhile, I was learning quite a bit. I was Warren's personal assistant, and it was an education to watch him operate. Cadle was much larger than any place I had ever worked. Warren was a great organizer and ran a taut ship. I drove for him, trouble-shot for him, bought radio and television time and answered much of his mail. It was some job.

Socially, Laura Lee and I were busier than we had ever been. We made lots of friends, attended their parties and helped entertain friends of the Tabernacle. Over Memorial Day, Warren always invited scores of people to the '500 race as his guests. I arranged for the post-race dinner at the Marriott Hotel.

It was a stimulating time for me. I felt I had finally hit the big time. With Warren's philosophy as an excuse, I went as far as the finance company would let me in being a first-class ambassador. I bought a Lincoln Continental and new clothes galore. We moved into a much more expensive home across from the carillon and lakes on the Butler University campus. None of these things were in our budget, but I didn't stop to consider that—I was "thinking big."

With all the activity, all the running and all the things we were attempting to accumulate, the deep hurt still festered inside Laura and me. A big car, a plush house and loud parties couldn't cure our diseased marriage.

Once, while Roy Burkhart of Columbus was conducting meetings in Anderson, we went down to visit my folks. Dr. Burkhart had written many practical books and was an adept counselor. Just how we got together I don't know—maybe Dad arranged it. In our conversation, I revealed some of my past indiscretions, and he offered some sound spiritual advice which I was in no way able to implement. However, I was moved by his understanding and compassion. So was Laura Lee.

I can still see her curled up like a small kitten in a huge, green leather chair. Dr. Burkhart, no doubt feeling sympathy for her after hearing my story, sat down on the arm of the chair and talked with her. I watched her eyes as he dealt with her gently and compassionately. When he excused himself to go to his room, he gave her hand a warm squeeze. A tear ran down her cheek. She was so hungry for someone to reach out to her in genuine love and understanding. I started toward her, but turned and went into the kitchen for a drink of water instead.

There is a postscript to the Roy Burkhart conversation. I had given him permission to use some of my story if he changed the names and situations. Laura Lee knew of the arrangement, so she was anxious to read what I had told him. Our communication was so poor that she hoped to learn something about me by reading this famous minister's book. All she found were several case histories of bizarre infidelity—none of which vaguely resembled anything that had happened to me. By this time, however, she was so suspicious that she was sure I was one of those he was describing in the book. The problem could have been solved by a phone call to Dr. Burkhart, except that, in the meantime, he had died. The suspicion and distrust tortured Laura and, by now, she was in a permanent fog.

So was I. The high style of living had created severe financial problems. Payments on the Lincoln were past due, and the bank was threatening to repossess it. We were also behind on several other loans, amounting to a debt of several thousand dollars. As the pressure built, my head infections were becoming more and more frequent, and I often retreated to bed where sympathy was forthcoming.

To help the financial situation, I began moonlighting as an insurance salesman. Leon Lawhead, a general agent with National Life of Vermont, took me under his wing and helped me get my broker's license. The company supplied me with $100.00 per week, which, when added to my salary from Cadle and the money Laura made as a part-time beautician, was more than we had ever made. Unfortunately, our outgo was still considerably more than our income, and it was all we could do to keep our heads above water.

When Warren Walker learned that I was selling insurance on the side, he was less than overjoyed. And although I don't know definitely that it led to my next dilemma, it may have figured in it.

In the summer of 1961, the annual international convention was being held in Anderson, about forty miles away. I was invited to sing.

"Mind if I drive over after the broadcasts each day?" I asked Warren.

"Better yet," he replied, "why not take the week off. I'd like to bring Jerry Barnes in from Texas." Jerry was a singer who had occasionally appeared on the program. I thought it was an ideal solution until I went in to get my check the following week.

"Sorry," Buford Cadle said. "Warren says you have been paid in full. You're through."

CHAPTER 11

Something Worth Living For

I was completely devastated by the announcement. Without any hint of warning, my two years of singing at Cadle were over. I thought I had mastered the art of knowing where I stood and when it was time to move on. Although I still had personal and spiritual problems which must have been reflected in my singing, I was genuinely pleased with my work. Singing six days a week on radio and Sundays on TV, I had gathered a large following and received many letters each week. I felt that these people really couldn't get along without me.

The final indignity was that it happened so suddenly, with no time for any face-saving moves. I wasn't leaving. I was fired—then, there, and finally.

My mind was a blur. I knew one thing for sure, though. If we were over our heads financially with the Cadle check coming in, we were really in trouble without it. We sold the car, most of our furniture, and moved back to Anderson. Some long-time friends, Glenn and Helena Sealock, gave us the use of their one-room, converted garage. Helena made a place in the house for the kids to sleep, and Laura and I slept in the garage. It was an impossible arrangement, but our options were either the Sealocks' garage or a tent, and I didn't have the money to buy a tent.

125

It was quite a comedown. Two months earlier, on Memorial Day weekend, I had arranged a plush affair at the Marriott Hotel where Warren's well-to-do friends had gathered for a post-race dinner. Laura and I had enjoyed shrimp cocktails, two-inch prime porterhouse steaks, flaming desserts—the choice selections on the menu. Now, we were eating hamburgers from an oilcloth-covered table in a one-room garage that doubled as dining room, bedroom and living room.

Once again, Dad and Polly came to our rescue. Polly took one look at our living quarters and hurried to find Dad.

"This will never do." Within a short time, he had made the down payment on a house, and we moved in with our few possessions and some things the folks scraped together.

We were less than six blocks from the parsonage, but it had been a long, bumpy road—High Point, Huntington, Detroit, Middletown, Chicago, Indianapolis and a lot of stops in between. I was not much richer or wiser for the journey.

Although I'm sure Leon Lawhead was not in favor of my representing his company in Anderson, he reluctantly okayed it. So I sold insurance by phone. My pay was now down to $75.00 a week. Laura Lee had gone back to work at Mary's beauty shop where she had been employed during college days. She didn't want to be away from the children all day, but we had no choice. We needed her paycheck. With her $40.00 per week added to my small income, we were managing, but I was becoming irrational.

One day in a rage, I pulled a .38 revolver out of the dresser drawer, picked up a Bible and waved them dramatically in Laura's face.

"I'm going into the bedroom," I said, "and either I'm going to find God or use this."

She looked at me soberly, then turned to see Paula staring, wide-eyed. Hurriedly, Laura led her out of the house.

It was not the first time I had threatened to take my life. Earlier, I had told Laura I was going to drive the car off a bridge and had sat on the porch for an hour or so, contemplating my next move. Finally, Laura, who had been waiting to serve my supper, brought a plate of food and put it beside me.

"There," she said. "Before you kill yourself, eat your supper."

This time, however, she believed I might be serious. She was outside praying fervently that she wouldn't hear a shot. Meanwhile, after a couple of minutes of Bible reading, I closed the book, lay down on the bed and closed my eyes.

An hour passed.

Two.

I woke to hear pounding on the door. I had gone to sleep, leaving Laura outside to wait the outcome.

A few days later, I was sitting in the house with a book in my hands. I couldn't concentrate enough to read. Laura was at work. I had locked the kids out of the house and wouldn't let them in even for a drink. As I sat there, totally miserable, the phone rang. It was Cliff Hutchinson, the pastor from Middletown, Ohio.

Throughout the story of my life, God has known when I most needed a friend and He has always sent that person along. At the time, I thought things were as bad as they could possibly be. I was to learn that they would get worse—a lot worse—before there would be a song in my heart. At this moment, God laid it on Cliff's heart to reach out to me in strength and compassion. I will always be grateful to Cliff for his willingness to be used.

"I've lost my minister of music, Doug," he told me, "and I'd like for you to come and help us out."

"Gee, I'd like to," I hesitated, searching for the right words, "but I'm all tied up in the insurance business." I said something about devoting full time to selling and couldn't possibly work anything else into my busy schedule.

The truth was that I was familiar with Cliff's church from my earlier assignment in Middletown at the Crawford Street Church of God. His services were unstructured, spontaneous and sometimes loud. Although some referred to this format as "being led by the Spirit," I didn't think it was a situation in which I would be comfortable.

Cliff had started the church and had enjoyed a successful ministry. Still, I had too much pride to want to be associated with it after my prestigious position at Cadle. However, when he mentioned a salary of $75.00 for Saturday night and Sunday, I decided I wasn't so busy after all. The next weekend, I began serving the Grand Avenue Church of God.

With the $75.00 coming in from the insurance company and my new source of income, I felt almost respectable again. My affluence was short-lived, however. The same week I started to work for Cliff, the insurance job came to an end. I wasn't making any sales that would justify my salary, and a decision was made to terminate my employment.

All the things I had heard about the services at Grand Avenue were true. At first, it bothered me that I couldn't work out a program for each service. No matter what I planned and rehearsed, Cliff would change his mind by the time we had finished the first song.

"That was wonderful, Doug," he would say. "You know, I would like to hear the choir sing 'Amazing Grace.'" He was sensitive to the Spirit, and he knew the people needed a warm, moving service to give them strength and courage for daily living.

And the people responded. It seemed that something dramatic happened in every service. A steady stream of needy people—alcoholics, teenagers, young couples—made their way forward and had their lives renewed. The church, under Cliff's ministry, maintained a constant spirit of optimism and expectancy.

As the weeks went by, I found myself asking again and again, "Why doesn't something happen to me?"

I began working at Grand Avenue Church in October of 1961. I was still there in January of the following year when Cliff conducted a week-long series of special meetings. Because the drive between Anderson and Middletown was two hundred miles round trip, I stayed with Cliff all week. Laura didn't mind. In fact, it was probably a relief to have me out of the house. After the Indianapolis dismissal, our relationship hit some new lows. What I didn't know was that Laura had come to the decision that it was time to call our marriage off. I don't know what I would have said if I had known what she was planning to do—try to change her mind, I suppose. I could not deny that she had plenty of cause, but, because there had been no dramatic event to tip the scales, her decision came unexpectedly. We hadn't had a big fight or any new or unusual problems. She had just finally come to the conclusion that, as bad as separation would be, there was no point in going on.

On Friday night of the meeting, the Sweet Chariots, an eighty-voice black choir, were to appear. Laura and some friends, Helena and Lloyd Lambert, came over to Middletown that night to hear the performance. Afterward, we had a cup of coffee and chatted amiably. Then she and our friends left for home.

"See you Sunday night," I said as she got in the car. She smiled and gave me a little wave. I was to remember that poignant, little wave many times in the future.

The week closed with a long, victorious service on Sunday night, and I was tired but happy as I made the two and one-half hour trip to Anderson. It was well past midnight when I parked in front of the house and started up the walk. From the outside, things looked normal. The lights were on, and I knew Laura would be watching TV and the girls would have long been in bed.

It's strange, but there is something about emptiness that can be felt. I was only two or three steps inside the door when I knew something was wrong. First of all, Tangy, our poodle reacted oddly. Instead of her usual warm greeting, she lay on the floor as though she were sick.

"What's wrong, Tangy?" She licked my hand.

"Laura," I called, and my voice, echoing, mocked me through the house.

"They're gone, aren't they, Tangy?" I walked through the rooms. Everything was in order. My shirts were hanging in the closet, freshly washed and pressed. The house was scrubbed and shining, as if someone were coming—or going.

When I walked into the bathroom, a neatly written note was taped to the mirror of the medicine chest. It is burned into my memory:

> Dear Doug,
>
> I've prayed about this for a year, asking God if I should leave you. I've concluded that it's the best thing to do. The kids are confused and are having trouble in school, and I'm afraid I'm losing my mind. I've got to try it alone. It's my only hope. Please try to understand. I won't ever criticize you to the children. I know you've tried, but I just can't go on anymore. Please don't come looking for me.
>
> Laura

In a daze, I walked into the living room and fell into a chair. It is impossible to describe the loneliness and despair that tumbled over me. The silence was almost unbearable and seemed to shout about all the times that I had demanded quiet from the girls. I made an effort to be angry:

"What's she trying to do?"

"How could she leave me?"

"What will people think?"

But the tender sadness of her note and my own guilt only intensified the awful reality. It had really happened, and it was my fault.

I don't know how long I sat there. Sometime later, I called Polly and Dad who were in California conducting meetings. To my surprise, they knew. Someone had already broken the news. Apparently, I was the *last* to know.

"I'm sorry," he said simply.

"Do you have any idea where she may have gone?" I asked. No, he didn't.

"Dad, what should I do?" I remember asking helplessly as I had once asked about a broken bike wheel. Once again, I turned instinctively to my parents and their unmoving faith for strength.

"Go to bed, and try to get some sleep. Things will look differently in the morning. We'll pray for you. Take a look at Romans 8:28. It's true."

We hung up and I was alone again. Reaching for my Bible, I found the verse: "And we know that all things work together for good to them that love God, to them who are called according to his purpose."

It was not much consolation. "God," I prayed, burying my head in my hands, "where do I go from here?"

While I was searching my soul that night in the lonely house, Laura and the girls were halfway through Kansas on their way to Denver and the home of Reverend and Mrs. Bert James. The Jameses were family friends. He had been the pastor of the church in Nebraska where Laura had made her decision for Christ.

Later, I was to learn the story of Laura's "sudden" decision and departure. In sharing our marital problems with Helena, Laura was told that she was more than justified in leaving me. On her way to the beauty shop Thursday morning of that week, she decided that Helena was right. Suddenly, she knew she could make it on her own. With the relief that comes with decision, she ran back to Helena's house and said, "I'm leaving Doug."

Helena was not surprised and offered to help. "Where are you going and when?"

"To Denver as soon as I can pack," was the quick reply.

Together, they laid some plans. On the weekend, while I was in Middletown, they packed a U-Haul trailer and the Sealock station wagon. On Sunday morning, they would be ready to start for Denver.

"Ellen Rich might like to go along," Helena suggested. "She could help with the driving."

Ellen was more than willing. I don't know what Ellen and Helena told their husbands, but neither of them seemed to know where the girls were going.

Other than the humiliation—I suppose that is the right word—of being left by one's wife, the thing that bothered me most was not knowing where she was. I wanted to talk to her, reason with her—but that is just what Laura didn't want. She was afraid I would be able to talk her out of going.

I began my detective work on Monday morning. Dean Nicholson had counselled with Laura, so I called there first. Nick had loaned her $50.00 but was reluctant to tell me where she had gone with the kids. It was Lloyd, who ran the Christian Center, who gave me the information I needed. He had helped her pack.

The news that she was going to be with the Jameses eased my mind somewhat, but I was still distraught. Denver was a thousand miles away. The thought of that many miles between us broke me up. In the car driving home from Lloyd's, the tears made it impossible to see, so I pulled over to the curb. I felt a huge emptiness and excruciating pain. Sitting there, utterly despondent, I thought of my gun. Suicide seemed a simple solution. I guess the only thing that kept me from shooting myself was knowing what the Bible says about taking one's life.

That afternoon, I called Cliff to tell him what had happened. We have an unwritten law among ministers that says those who have broken homes should not serve until their estrangement is mended.

"I guess you'll have to get along without me, friend, until this thing is worked out."

"What do you mean?" he asked.

"I know I can't work for the church while Laura and I are separated."

"Are you in any new trouble here?"

"No," I replied.

"Well, then, you're still my minister of music."

I couldn't believe he was serious. I expected him to say that I should quit immediately and that, at the most, he would be praying for me. But, instead, he said something I'll never forget.

"I knew you had problems when I called you over here. But we needed a minister of music, and you needed love and spiritual guidance. I felt that God wanted me to get the two together, and I still think that's what He wants."

"But you know you will be greatly criticized when they find out about our separation," I persisted.

"That's what the church is for, Doug," Cliff continued, "to help those who need help."

I was moved to tears. He was reaching out to me as I had seen him do for others so many times. It was a ray of light in a dark tunnel.

By Tuesday, I was able to reach Laura by phone. It was a strained conversation, but I sensed a new confidence in her voice. She had found a job shortly after arriving in Denver. Her former employer, Bill Anderson, now had a beauty shop in Colorado Springs. He offered her a job that would more than care for her financial needs. In spite of that, I felt my responsibility and told her I would send her money right away. She had also found a place to stay in the basement apartment of a family in Rev. James' church.

Near the end of the call, I said, "I want you to come back."

"No, I'm afraid not." Her voice was calm, but firm.

"I miss you."

She didn't reply to that, and when I said, "I'm sorry," she thanked me. It was apparent that it had been a very painful decision to make the move, but now that she had made it, she refused to go through it again.

I was more discouraged than ever after the call. Somehow, I had thought I could persuade Laura to return. Now, it seemed there was no hope of ever having my family back.

On Wednesday morning, Cliff called early to say that he had fixed a room at the church and that I was welcome to use it anytime I wanted. I decided I might as well take him up on his offer. There, I could work and maybe divert my mind from my troubles part of the time. It seemed that every day my depression grew worse. I was desperate. Something had to happen. What I didn't know was that at long last, I was in sight of home—I didn't have far to run now.

Thursday afternoon, I headed toward Middletown for the evening service. I was driving on Route 122 east of Eaton. The Volkswagen could do 83 miles an hour, and I had my foot flat on the floorboard. It was a bitterly cold day with an angry, gray sky. Dirty white snow from the week before was piled high beside the highway. The day was a perfect background for my mood.

My mind was totally occupied with the tattered remains of my life. My thoughts hopscotched from one memory to another—the two times I got kicked out of school . . . the churches I had let down . . . the friends I had disappointed . . . the women I had used . . . my insensitivity to Laura . . . my meanness to the girls . . .

But there was a difference in my thinking. I was finally admitting that *I* had made a mess of my life. No longer was I blaming the church or my parents or the school or Laura or anybody else. Like the prodigal son, I had come to myself. I started to pray, I mean really pray:

"God, what a mess I've made of everything. My life up to now has been useless. When I think of all the opportunities

I have had and how I have blown them all, I see how worthless I really am. If you're still there, let me know it. I've gone about as far as I can go. I don't even have the desire to continue. Please give me something worth living for . . ."

Suddenly, I realized I had gone into a sharp turn too fast. A speed limit sign—35 miles per hour—had flashed by. And I was doing nearly 80. The car was leaning so far that Tangy was clawing on the side window trying to get a foothold. The car slid onto the shoulder, just on the verge of rolling into the ditch. I had lost control completely.

"This is it," I thought. "The end . . ."

In that instant I had an unbelievable awareness that God loved me still and that if I died I would go to be with Him. In that runaway car, sliding through the dirt, snow and gravel, the deepest peace I had ever known swept over me.

Then a second miracle happened. The God who knew how to fill my heart with peace also knew how to drive a Volkswagen, and all four wheels returned to the ground. I steered the car back onto pavement. In a mile or so I found a place to pull off the road, and I stopped and bowed my head. Peace, warmth, joy pulsed through my whole being.

I still didn't know what the future held for my home. There were years of failures to live down. There would be long, agonizing hours of counseling ahead. It was to be awhile before I was sure what God wanted me to do and how He would help me bring it about. But this much I did know—for the first time in my life, I was on the right road.

CHAPTER 12

Through It All

I arrived in Middletown late in the afternoon. Cliff was in the study at the church. I was eager to share the things that had happened on the way up. When I had finished my story, including the close scrape, he laughed out loud and asked, "So what do you make of it all?"

"I think I've been saved," I said.

"Well, it's about time." He was so genuinely happy for me that I was aware again of what a true Christian and friend he was to me.

"What should I do tonight?" I asked. "Should I tell the people everything that has happened, including the separation?"

"Not necessarily. You should just be willing to share as He leads you." Cliff believed strongly in the leadership of the Holy Spirit and he knew that if I would let Him guide me I would do and say the right thing.

We went out for a bite of supper. When we returned to the church, the seats were already beginning to fill. The sanctuary held nearly five hundred people, and even the midweek service was well attended.

After the congregational singing, some Scripture and a prayer, Cliff called on the ushers to take the offering. While they were passing the plates, I sang Ira Stanphill's song, "I Know Who Holds Tomorrow":

> *I don't know about tomorrow,*
> *I just live from day to day.*
> *I don't borrow from its sunshine,*
> *For its skies may turn to gray.*
> *I don't worry o'er the future,*
> *For I know what Jesus said,*
> *And today I'll walk beside Him,*
> *For He knows what is ahead.*

As I was singing, a young girl near the back of the church left her seat, walked down the aisle and knelt at the altar. No invitation had been given nor did the song really have an invitational message. But I could feel the power of the Spirit through me as I sang. During the second verse, another person joined the girl kneeling at the altar, and half a dozen more were on the way.

By the time I had finished the song, about forty people were praying earnestly at the front of the church. I was more certain than ever that what happened to me on the road to Middletown was real. Like Paul on the way to Damascus, I had seen the light. Seldom had anyone responded to my singing in this way. I had always tried to set a good mood for the preacher, but there was never any real power in my message. I wasn't even singing better than usual. It was just that, for the first time, my spirit was witnessing with His Spirit, and the truth flowed through me with conviction and power. I was soon to begin a serious study of the ways of the Spirit. The first lesson was the subtle difference between singing to be good and singing to be used. After one song, I knew I didn't want to go back to the old way again.

Cliff went to the pulpit as I sat down and said, "I think you can all tell that something very wonderful happened to Doug today. I was going to preach, but I would rather have him tell you what he told me this afternoon in the study. Doug, would you tell us what the Lord did for you today?"

I stood and began talking. I told them about my life—the problems I had had as a kid, my trouble in college, our marital difficulties, including Laura's decision to leave me.

"I was convinced that I had nothing to live for. I came to the end of myself and found that God was there. He moved in to tell me I was still His child and that He had never stopped loving me. He did that this afternoon." Then, I told them about the near-accident.

By the time I had finished, others were coming forward to pray. I had never felt more unburdened, more clean in my life. Confession had always been a disagreeable word to me. It was almost as if God wanted to use the past to embarrass me. Now, the true meaning of the words, "If we confess our sins, he is faithful and just to forgive . . ." broke in upon me. Anything we won't admit, we are saddled with; but, everything we confess, He forgives and takes away.

Apparently, scores of others were carrying a heavy load of guilt and need just as I had been. As they, too, opened themselves to the forgiveness of God, the service became a celebration—a festival of joy!

The service finally came to a close. Cliff looked at me across the platform and raised a hand in victory. "Well, praise the Lord!" he shouted. I was too choked up to answer.

When the last car had pulled away and Cliff and I were the only ones left in the church, he went into the study to call Laura. He wanted her to share my experience and the great service that had just concluded.

She listened patiently but was unmoved. "I've seen Doug turn a corner so many times, I'm dizzy. I just can't believe it until I've seen it work for a long, long time."

He must have talked to her an hour. He told her that he had seen many changed people in his ministry and that he was convinced that God had really touched me. Laura wanted desperately to believe, but she still had reservations. Too many things had happened too many times.

I desperately wanted a chance to try again with God as the head of our home. But I was doubtful that I would ever have the opportunity. Many times during the next couple of weeks, I awakened in the middle of the night with a recurring "nightmare" that Laura would not come back. Still, I didn't give up. I pleaded with God to speak to her heart. I read the Bible several hours a day, especially J. B. Phillips' translation. In my reading, I came across the word "fasting" and its spiritual uses. I began to fast and pray that, somehow, God would put our home back together.

During this period of prayer, Bible reading and fasting, one of the directions I received was to find a counselor, but I didn't know whom I should see. One day, Lloyd Lambert mentioned that Dr. Bert Coody, an outstanding Christian psychologist in Anderson, had helped him solve some problems. An hour later, I talked with Dr. Coody and he agreed to see me. He was able to help me on a very practical level in several sessions.

Meanwhile, some of the ministers in our conference had heard of my conversion and invited me to come sing and tell my story. I was willing to go for two reasons. First, I wanted to tell what God had done for me. Secondly, I was broke and thousands of dollars in debt. The Volkswagen people were ready to repossess the car. We had been in deep financial difficulty even before Laura left. Now, with my sending her $30.00 to $40.00 weekly out of the $75.00 the church was paying me, I was losing ground fast.

Henry Howard, an associate minister at the church, knew I needed work. He took me with him to a week-long meeting in Evandale, just outside of Cincinnati. When the week was over, he gave me a rather large check, saying that it was my share of the offering. Several years later, I learned that he had given me all the money and had paid the expenses of driving over a hundred miles a day out of his own pocket. That Monday, I put some extra money in the envelope I sent to Laura.

Because it was so hard to know what to say in a letter, I began to send contemporary greeting cards with the checks. The cards were humorous, but the verse often carried a pointed message.

One said, "You could be replaced by a computer."

Another read, on the outside: "I like you a lot . . ." and, on the inside: "better from a distance."

Laura responded by sending me "message" cards, too. It was the only communication between us for several weeks, but it was a start. I was afraid the longer we were apart, the more easily it could become permanent. This form of communication was better than none at all.

Laura had been away for better than a month when I was asked to sing for the Holiness Indoor Camp Meeting at Evansville. I was afraid to go because I was sure they didn't know about my broken home. I prayed about it and decided God wanted me to go.

Clyde Dupin was the pastor of the host church. Our opening service went well, but I hesitated to share the things that were happening to me.

That evening, however, I told Clyde and was amazed by his sympathetic reaction. He rejoiced with me in my new relationship with God and pledged to pray earnestly with me for God to work out our tangled lives.

Somehow, I think I was surprised that people would still accept and forgive me after they knew what I had done and been. I guess that same fear kept me from being honest with God all those years. I just couldn't believe that He, Who knew the whole story all along, was still reaching out to me in love and forgiveness.

Laura and the girls were continually on my mind. As I drove back and forth from Anderson to Evansville that week, I was praying earnestly that God would help me get them back. Late one night, on the way home, a voice spoke to me so clearly that I almost looked around to see if someone else was in the car.

"She may not come back. But even if you have to go on without her, I will be with you."

Suddenly the realization came to me that when He said, "I will never leave you nor forsake you," He was talking to me. As the tears coursed down my cheeks, I answered from the depths of my soul,

"I have given my life to you, and I will let you lead. Regardless of the outcome of my marriage, I will serve you." A new peace flooded me, and I was prepared to continue with or without Laura.

We had been apart almost eight weeks. Laura had moved to Denver on January 21. It was the middle of March when I decided to call once more to persuade her to come home.

"How are you?" I asked when I heard her voice at the other end of the line.

"Fine." Her voice was a mixture of warmth and reserve.

"And the girls. How are they?"

"They're just great. They really like school."

After we had chatted a couple of minutes, I mustered my courage for the big question and asked, "When are you coming home?"

"I'm not sure I am," she replied.

"Well, what are you going to do?"

"I don't know yet."

"We're going to have to decide soon," I pressed.

"You decide then. I have to go now."

"Wait," I insisted. "I want to see you, talk with you. Will you let me see you?"

"It won't do any good, Doug. It's better this way, I think."

"I can come out tomorrow, just for a couple of days."

"No, I'd prefer that you didn't."

"Please," I pleaded.

There was a long pause. Finally, "It's an awfully long drive for nothing, Doug. If you feel you must come, I'll see you, but I won't go home with you. You should know that—I'm not kidding."

That evening I saw Steele Smith at Warner Press and borrowed $200.00. Early the next morning, I backed the car out of the drive and pointed it toward Denver, eleven hundred miles away. Since I had to be back by Sunday to sing at Middletown, I intended to drive straight through. This would give me Friday with Laura. I planned to head back early Saturday.

Mid-March is usually a cold month in the plains, and it was especially frigid outside. Inside, the Volks heater made the temperature toasty and I was feeling good, singing with the radio by the hour. Illinois and Missouri fell behind me and, soon, I was racing across Kansas. I was making great time, and my anticipation of seeing Laura was growing by the mile. Although she had said she would not come back with me, I prayed all the way that I could make her change her mind. As I drove along, that hope kept me going. I had set a goal of averaging sixty miles an hour. By midnight, I was in mid-Kansas, averaging better than sixty-five. Wherever traffic would permit, I'd open it up.

Then, about 1:00 A.M., I heard the fly wheel go. It had happened before, so I recognized the familiar thumping sound. I looked in the rear-view mirror and saw the red light on top of the grain elevator in the last town. It must have been twenty miles back. Ahead, the red light marking the next elevator in the next town appeared to be about the same distance. I just barrelled on, hoping to make it.

I made it and drove right up on the grease rack at the first and only gas station. I turned the key, but the Volks was so hot, it just kept running. I shifted into gear and, reluctantly, the motor quit.

I explained my problem to the gray-haired attendant. He shook his head negatively.

"I don't think you can get any help this time of the night."

"Where's the next Volkswagen dealer?"

"One hundred and five miles."

"When's the next bus west?"

"Ten A.M."

"Oh, man," I groaned. "I've got to get to Denver in a hurry. Is there anybody around who could spotweld the fly wheel for me? I could probably coax the car to Denver and have it replaced there."

The man shook his head again. "Mac Thomas has a welding rig, but he's forty miles away. Last time I called him out on an emergency, he was madder than a hornet by the time he got here, and he told me not to call him in the middle of the night again."

He went out to pump gas into a car that had just pulled in, and I sat down in the car. "Lord," I prayed, "surely You wouldn't bring me this far for nothing. Please help me. Show me what to do."

My head was still in my hands against the steering wheel when the attendant yelled out of his office, "Man, are you in luck! Here comes Mac now."

I climbed out of the car and looked outside. There, with "Mac Thompson Welding" painted on the side, was a truck pulling into the station. I rushed out to the front door of the truck and wasted no time in launching into my story. The driver pushed the bill of his red plaid work cap off his forehead and lifted his ear-tabs in order to hear over the whistling wind. Finally, he squinted his blue eyes and shook his head, motioning me toward the door. I followed him inside.

"Now, start over," he said. "What's your problem?"

I began again. "I'll pay you whatever you want. I've got to get to Denver. My wife and three kids are living there. I just have twenty-four hours to talk them into coming home with me, then I have to start back to my job. If I don't get this fly wheel fixed, I won't even get there."

For the first time, Mac smiled. "I once went through something like that, he said. "it's a pretty rough feelin'. Sure, I'll fix your fly wheel."

"I'll help," I volunteered.

"Tell ya what," he said. "I'm about asleep on my feet. Got called out on an emergency. Go over to the diner and get me a cup of coffee."

By the time I got back, he had his tools out and was well into the repair job. Thirty minutes later, I was ready to roll.

"How much do I owe you?" I asked.

"Forget it. Hope ya get things patched up with the missus," he answered with a wave and ambled back toward his truck.

"Thank you, God, for Mac." Once again, in the middle of the night, in a place where help was least likely, God had provided everything I needed. With renewed courage, I pointed the car west on Route 36 and pressed the accelerator to the floor.

It was about 5:00 A.M. when I reached the outskirts of Denver—nineteen hours after I had pulled out of Anderson. It took me another hour to find the address. A night light illuminated the steps leading down to the basement entrance. A sign read, "Merry Widow Retreat."

I paused before I knocked. Eight weeks was a long time. I wanted so badly to take Laura and the girls home with me. Still, as I stood there in the cold morning air, I remembered her firm, cool refusal to consider it.

I knocked softly. A light came on inside, and Laura came to the door. We stood there for a moment, neither of us knowing what to say or do.

"Come in," she said, taking my coat. "How was your trip?" She had busied herself in the kitchen with the coffee after our awkward pause.

"Long," I sighed, wearily.

"You must be dead."

I had been anxiously looking for some sign that she still cared, and the concern in her voice was like music to my ears. I noticed something else. Even though she had just gotten out of bed, her hair was combed and pretty. Through all our troubles, she had kept herself looking neat and stylish, but I wanted to believe that she had fixed her hair for me. Now, as I sat across from her in the early morning light, my mind turned to our dating days in college. She was just as dainty and pretty and lovable now as then. What had happened? Why had I turned from Laura in search of companionship elsewhere? How had I failed to see what a beautiful person she was inside and out?

We talked about the girls who were still sleeping and about our own lives. She told me a little about the town and church, and I told her about the things that had been happening to me. Finally, I could bear it no longer and asked impulsively, "Please, will you and the girls come home with me?"

"I just don't believe I can go back to the kind of life we had before," came her wistful reply.

"It's not the same," I insisted, "I've changed!"

"Doug, I've seen you 'change' and start over a hundred times. I know you really mean to try, but it just never works."

"You'll have to trust me," I said.

I told her about Bert Coody's counseling and that I believed I was beginning to understand myself and what made me do the things I had done. With God's help, they were forever behind.

The separation had been painful for Laura, too. She told me she had not been able to read or even watch TV, because the conflicts in almost every story revived all the old hurts and wounds of our marriage. And she would cry until there were no tears left.

"I picked up a copy of 'The Late Liz' by Gertrude Behanna," Laura said. "I couldn't put it down. The author told about her life and how nothing made sense until she really put Christ in every decision. I asked myself if I had really done His will, or if I had just given up too soon by breaking off with you. I am still not sure."

Laura had been stunned by a passage in Matthew where Jesus was asked why Moses was given the law of divorce. Jesus' answer was, "Because of the hardness of your heart." This statement had frightened her.

"I don't want to live the rest of my life that way. I don't want to be a hard, cold person. But whether I can live with you again is something I can't answer."

"Will you try?" I pleaded. "I want you and the kids back with all my heart. I promise things will be different."

Suddenly, she was in my arms and, with the tears flowing down our faces, words were no longer necessary. In our hearts we knew we could begin again. We woke the kids, and the five of us rejoiced that we were going to be a family once more.

I rented a U-Haul and we began packing. How much of our lives have revolved around a rented trailer! Laura had worked hard fixing up the basement apartment. Once in a while, she would stop packing and pause to ponder something. I could tell she was still struggling with her decision. She wanted to come back, but she was afraid it wouldn't work and she would have to endure the whole thing again.

It was nearly five o'clock when we drove to the parsonage to tell the Jameses of our decision. They seemed to have some misgivings.

"I think you're rushing things. Laura needs more time to work this out," Bert said.

"She's going home with me," I said firmly.

"I hope you're both doing the right thing." Bert looked at me as if he felt I had pressured Laura.

Laura was beginning to look as if she were having second thoughts, too, so I quickly backed the trailer up to the garage where more of Laura's things were stored. By 6:30, we had finished packing and were ready to leave.

"You haven't eaten yet, have you?" Bert asked. "Let us buy your dinner."

I didn't really want to eat with them. Bert's cautious manner frightened me. But Laura wanted a farewell meal with them, so we agreed to meet them at a restaurant which was on our way out of town. After eating, we said our goodbyes and loaded the kids into the car. By 8:30 we were on our way. But we were not home free yet.

The 5' x 8' trailer was a big load for the Volks under the best of circumstances. However, once you got rolling, it could make fifty-five or sixty miles per hour. After an hour or so, we began to lose speed. At first, I thought I might have left the emergency brake on. I discovered that the reason for the reduced speed was a rapidly rising headwind. A wind of fifty miles per hour added to the heavy load we were carrying resulted in a stalemate. Out on the plains, there is nothing to break the wind, and we took it full force, the trailer acting as a sail pulling us in the opposite direction. Finally, we were creeping along at only ten-fifteen miles per hour in second.

About midnight, I told Laura, "I'm afraid the Lord's trying to tell us something. You know, if we break down out here in the middle of nowhere, we could freeze to death." I put my coat over Dee Dee, now three, who was sleeping in the back seat with Paula and Karen. Laura was in a frightened daze.

"Maybe we're doing the wrong thing. Maybe I should take you back," I said. "What do you think?"

"I don't know," she said hesitantly.

"I think I'll call Bert and see what he advises."

A funny expression crossed her face. I knew she was thinking I had never asked for advice before. Maybe I had changed after all.

At the next town, which was only a wide spot in the road,

I pulled off the road and into a tavern parking lot. I asked the bartender if I could use the phone. He pointed to a phone on the wall in the corner.

"Could I have some change?" I called, over the music blaring from the jukebox.

"Sure." The man took my dollar to the cash register.

Finally, I reached Bert. "I need your advice."

"What?"

The noise and the raucous music made it difficult to hear. Cupping my hands around the receiver, I tried again. After several attempts, he got the message—we had run into some bad weather and were considering returning to Denver.

"I think God is trying to tell me something," I shouted.

"What?"

"God is trying to tell me something," I shouted again. "We've come only about a hundred miles in four hours. Trailers are being blown over, trucks are in the ditch, signs are being knocked down. The wind must be blowing fifty miles an hour."

"We've been praying since you left," Bert said. "I don't really know what to tell you. Why not pull into a motel and see how you feel in the morning."

"Thanks, Bert. That's a good idea."

Fifteen miles down the road, we found a motel. Our money was dangerously low so we had planned to drive straight through. One by one, I carried the children into the motel room and tucked them in. Their peaceful sleep went unbroken. Laura was tense and wakeful. The full gamut of emotions which we had experienced during the eventful day had taken their toll. Dead tired, we needed sleep, yet the turmoil still swirled about us, making rest impossible.

Taking my family back to Denver was the last thing I wanted to do. "But if that's what you want me to do, God, I'll do it." Finally, Laura dropped off to sleep and I pulled the bedspread over her. I sat in a chair, dozing off for a few minutes, then waking with a start. I don't know how much I slept. It was a confused, miserable night.

Early the next morning, I peeked out the window, saw that the wind was still blowing hard and that it was beginning to snow. The wind was driving the snow horizontally. It would be impossible to drive, I thought. Then something else occurred to me.

I woke Laura quickly, shouting, "It's snowing. We've got to get out of here." I didn't know what direction we would be taking—back to Denver or on toward Indiana, but I knew our money would not permit us to be snowed in for several days.

She got the kids dressed and took them next door to the little restaurant for milk and sweet rolls while I gassed the car. The wind was unbelievable.

"We're in for a big snow," the station attendant said.

"Yeah, and I'm trying to fight that wind back to Indiana."

"Well, you're in luck," he said with a smile. "Now, last night you couldn't have made it with the rig you're pulling, but today, with the wind at your back . . ."

"At my back?" I checked directions and turned west toward Denver. The snow lashed my face with such force that it took my breath. The wind had changed! It had completely reversed itself! We didn't have to go back to Denver. I could take Laura and the girls home!

I saw them coming across the parking lot, running against a wind that seemed determined to keep them from me. It was as if they were suspended, moving in slow motion. I wanted to run to them, sweep them into my arms—but my feet wouldn't move, and my shouts were driven back into my throat. When they reached the car, I helped them inside. Circling to the other side, I climbed behind the wheel and started the motor.

"Sweetheart, the wind has shifted. It's at our back. We're going home."

For the first time since we left Denver, Laura smiled. Her

whole face became beautifully alive. Tears of overwhelming joy formed in her eyes and, as tenderly as I can ever recall, she leaned over and kissed me. For a second all was quiet, then dabbing her eyes with a tissue, she straightened up and said "Then what are waiting for? Let's go home."

A cheer rose from the girls in the back seat as I pulled away. The Volks hesitated only a second, and the big U-Haul trailer moved forward slowly. When the wind took hold, there was no stopping us.

We were going home, driven by a heaven-sent wind, and eighty miles-per-hour wind, that didn't quit until we were well into Illinois.

Do I really believe the wind was God-sent? Let me put it this way: I don't think God sends a damaging wind of that velocity just to push one little Volkswagen back to Indiana. I can't say whether the wind would have shifted anyway or not that night, but I do know we could not have made it home if it hadn't. Some may call it coincidence, but to us it was God saying loud and clear He had a special place in his heart for struggling, young couples with large trailers and small cars who have many miles to go and not much money.

And we have been giving Him the credit ever since for the good things that have come our way.

CHAPTER 13
A Rich Man Am I

Tangy was the first to greet us when we finally pulled into Anderson late the night of the great blow. She heard us drive in and was barking her hello long before we got to the door. When she saw me, she went into her ballerina-like dance, jumping on tiptoes, barking, wagging her tail. She and I had been through some significant incidents within a few short weeks. Her woebegone actions had first warned me that the house was empty and the family gone. Tangy was with me when we narrowly escaped a serious accident in the Volks on the way to Middletown. Now, here she was on hand for the family's homecoming.

Tangy was no happier to see us, though, than we all were to see her and the house. The girls scrambled to hug and pet her. Paula had huge, elephant tears in her eyes.

"Are you glad to be home?" I asked.

"Yes, Daddy, oh yes," she sighed.

Laura didn't say a word; she just gave my hand a gentle squeeze, and I looked at her. Tears of joy were flowing down our cheeks, and words were neither possible nor necessary. We believed that God would help us put our marriage back together, and we were determined to help Him.

Still, resolving to start again with a clean slate and actually making it work on a daily basis were different matters. There were times in the weeks ahead that the nursery rhyme "Humpty Dumpty" seemed to have been written about us:

Humpty Dumpty sat on a wall,
Humpty Dumpty had a great fall.
All the king's horses and all the king's men
Couldn't put Humpty together again.

There were so many pieces that were broken and scarred. The habits and attitudes we had accumulated through the years haunted us. Many areas of conflict needed changing, and the healing of our relationship came gradually—in steps and inches.

For almost eleven years, I had run roughshod over Laura's opinions and feelings. Insensitively and selfishly, I had done what I wanted—almost without exception—with little or no consideration for her. There is something to be said for strong, positive, decisive husbands; but my behavior was inexcusable. I had caused Laura to lose all confidence in herself.

In consulting with Dr. Coody, I began to see what a tyrant I had been. Though I had been hard-pressed to pay him for one visit a week, I knew I needed help and found his advice to be of immeasurable value. When Laura came back, she began to see him also in private sessions. She, too, found his wise counsel full of helpful insight. We both agree that God used Dr. Coody in a very significant way to rebuild our marriage. Although what we learned about ourselves in these sessions was sometimes traumatic, each new truth was a building block in our relationship.

What Laura needed most was to regain some feeling of self-respect and self-esteem. I had stripped her of both. Dr. Coody suggested that she needed to be more assertive, to challenge me if I tried my old bulldogging tactics. A gentle, rather introverted person by nature, Laura found this difficult to do after so many years of passive agreement. At the same time, Dr. Coody was telling me that I should listen to her—both to what she said and what she felt. One day while I was shaving, she came to the bathroom door to ask me about buying the girls some new shoes. As she talked, I noticed that her hands were shaking. I began to realize the extent to which I had intimidated her.

Gradually, through prayer, through Dr. Coody's counsel, through Bible study, devotions and church friends, we made progress. Once, a few weeks after we returned from Denver, I so provoked Laura that she threw a suitcase at me. Strangely enough, it cleared the air between us. I understood that she was upset, and we were able to discuss the problem. When Laura reported the incident to Dr. Coody, he roared with approving laughter. "Good for you, girl!"

My self-understanding grew with each counseling session. Though I paid for only one hour a week, Dr. Coody invited me to come as often as I wished. Sometimes, I was in his study as often as three or four times a week. It was genuinely exciting to learn why I had behaved so abominably, to look at my actions objectively and to weigh them rationally. I spent nearly one hundred hours counseling with him. How grateful I am for Dr. Coody and others like him. Dr. Clyde Narramore is another friend who comes to mind who has made a great contribution in this field. Not only are these people professionals in the highest sense of the word, but their faith gives them added power to help others deal with their problems from a Christian perspective.

In my case, I was able to see how I was blaming my parents unfairly for some things that were not their fault. How cruelly ungrateful I had been for their prayers and their love and I had failed to take my rightful responsibility as an adult. Dr. Coody helped me understand that, in my efforts to please my parents and live up to their standards, I had sublimated my real feelings. I had buried my hostility and rebelled against them indirectly, behaving in a self-destructive manner outside the home. It was my way of getting even.

Of course, each incident brought more guilt and more pressure. In the long run, I was hurting myself most of all. When I married Laura, she and the children became the victims of my left-over immaturity.

Dr. Coody was an entirely non-directive counselor, helping me to draw my own conclusions from the facts that were revealed to him. One method he used was to play a game about an imaginary family gathered around a table. The characters included a father, a mother, a son, daughter and a mysterious stranger. He told me to name the characters and to include myself as one of them. I found a place for everyone except myself. I took the role of the stranger.

"What's wrong with that setup?" Bert asked.

"I don't know." I was puzzled.

"Think about it. We will pick up at this point next session."

Later in the week we repeated the exercise. Suddenly I saw the paradox. I had three daughters myself but had never looked at myself as a father. And though I saw my father in his role, I didn't see myself as his son. Because I hadn't been able to live up to his expectations and because I couldn't accept my imperfections, I felt I wasn't worthy to be called his son. Over the years it had carried over into my spiritual life as well, since I couldn't feel I was worthy to be God's son either.

Little by little, Laura and I were progressing toward maturity. Learning to trust me again was the most difficult for her, I'm sure. In her weaker moments, doubt crept in and, from time to time, she had misgivings about her decision in coming back to me. However, the fact that God was now the head of our home made all the difference.

On another level, our financial situation could not have been worse. Polly and Dad again came to our rescue. When I recall how many times they helped us with love, prayer and sacrifice, it is hard to imagine how ungrateful I was at the time.

Dad borrowed $2000.00 to get us on our feet. In order to cut our obligations to the bone, we had returned everything that we had been buying on time. I guess the kids missed the TV more than anything. My total income of $75.00 per week came from the church at Middletown. Cliff and I discussed my joining him full-time, but that was a financial burden the church wasn't ready to bear. Nevertheless, he was persistent in trying to bring it about.

I was interested in a full-time job with the church mainly because of our financial struggle. But I had some inner doubts that it was the right direction for me to go. These inner stirrings—the first evidence that God might have something else in mind for me—caused me to begin petitioning the Lord for career guidance.

What He seemed to be saying in those first months after I came to know Him was, "Be patient. I have a plan for you and, when the time comes, I will reveal it to you."

Meanwhile, I continued to sing—on the Christian Brotherhood Hour each week and, occasionally, at special week-long meetings. I also recorded an album entitled "Songs That Lift the Heart" on the Twin-D label. Wherever I went to sing, I always carried a box of records under the front seat of the Volkswagen—just in case anyone asked for a copy. That box of fifty records was very often a three month's supply.

Three months passed. By June, I had several meetings lined up for the summer months. Several dates were with Dad; others were with Dave Grubbs and Henry Howard. Our first engagement was a week in Olympia, Washington. That trip stands out as a big turning-point in our lives. First, it was like a second honeymoon. Laura and I left the kids and the dog in Nebraska with Grandma Makings and headed toward the West Coast with stopovers at Estes Park, Denver, Yellowstone and Cortelane, Idaho. We had our problems on the way out—Laura got the mumps, and the valves on the car went out in Idaho. We had to make more stops than we had planned, and our money dwindled; but nothing could dampen our spirits. For the first time, we were both convinced that our marriage was definitely going to survive. Day by day on the trip, we sensed a healing presence. When the car broke down, we laughed about it. When Laura came down with the mumps, she bore the discomfort with a smile. I had more control over my emotions and no longer exploded when something went wrong.

We were both praying daily that God would show us what He wanted me to do. One day, while at the meetings with Polly and Dad in Washington, Laura asked, "Doug, what would you like most to do?"

"I think I'd like to travel," I replied. "I'd like to tell folks everywhere what the Lord has done for me. But I don't think I could make a living that way. No other singer in our denomination with a family to support has ever made it. It's too expensive for most churches to bring in an evangelist and a singer too."

She listened thoughtfully, then said, "Doug, if that's your heart's sincere desire, the Lord will find a way."

Your "heart's sincere desire"—that was a phrase I recognized as one of Glenn Clark's favorite expressions.

"But it would mean some real sacrifices. We'd be hard-pressed financially, and I'd be away from home for weeks at a time . . ."

"We'll manage," Laura said quietly.

I knew she was right. All the places I had been and all the traveling I had done began to fit into place—God had been leading me all along—maybe He wanted to be a traveling gospel singer.

A few days later, Cliff called to say that the board at Middletown had voted to hire me full-time.

"Cliff, you don't know how much I appreciate the offer. But I've been discussing the matter with the Lord, and He has something else in mind for me. I'm going on the road."

We talked about the problems, the insecurity, the hardships, as well as the blessings. "I may be making a mistake . . ."

"Nonsense! If you've prayed this thing through, the Lord won't let you fall. You're about to take the biggest step of faith in your life, buddy. You'll not be sorry. God bless you . . . and I'll be praying for you."

Cliff's encouragement was a great boost. Other things were beginning to happen, also. In Washington, as in other places, my testimony and song were being used by God to change lives. People came, pouring out their stories of misery and guilt. My witness—homely and halting as it was—was reaching people for the Lord. There was no explanation except that, deep inside, I was different, and that difference was coming through to others. Not all the spiritual growth was mine, however.

One morning, while we were in Olympia, Laura woke me with some exciting news. Though outwardly she and Polly had been very close, Laura had harbored some resentments deep within. It was a typical mother-in-law, daughter-in-law thing, really. Laura sensed some condescension; Polly was only trying to be helpful. She did not really believe she was interfering.

Because of this, Laura had developed great guilt feelings. She had prayed for years about these feelings, believing they were sinful and barriers to spiritual growth. But nothing changed. Then came that unforgettable morning in Olympia when she awoke and exclaimed, "It's gone!"

"What's gone?" I asked sleepily.

"My resentment of Polly. I couldn't sleep last night, so I got up and used the time praying that God would remove this terrible burden from me. I finally went back to bed and dropped off to sleep with the problem still unresolved. But, this morning, I feel clean and new. It's really gone," she said wonderingly.

We left Washington with several things settled. We knew our marriage was to be one of rich, spiritual unity; Laura had won a personal battle with resentment; I was in control of my immature emotions and was off all drugs. After my life-changing experience on the road to Middletown, I had quit using dexedrine entirely. I no longer needed or wanted it. The other negatives in my life seemed to vanish, too. I did not want to stay in bed in the mornings, trying to conjure up some imaginary illness which would give me an excuse not to get up and face the day. As my friend, Bob Harrington, the chaplain from Bourbon Street, says, I quit saying, "Good Lord—morning!" and began saying, "Good morning, Lord!"

But the greatest thing of all was that, for the first time in my life, I didn't have to run! I had a direction to go and adventure to pursue that were ordained and inspired by God. There is nothing quite as thrilling in life as knowing where you came from, why you're here and where you're going. Now, I had the answer to all three questions. Though materially I didn't have two nickels to rub together, I could say, "A rich man am I!"

I Don't Live There Anymore

The Volks was making those threatening noises again. I was a few miles outside of St. Louis, Michigan north of Lansing. Racing up Route 27, I was praying that God would help me get there before the motor gave out completely. It would mean another repair bill before I started home. The valves were burned so that the engine had lost most of its compression, and every hill dared us to try it. My doubts persisted right up to the city limits of St. Louis. As we rolled into town, I breathed a sigh of relief and a prayer of thanks to God. I believe that it is right to give thanks for all things, even sputtering car engines. However, at that particular moment, I was having some difficulty doing that. The thought of a $200.00 valve job at Christmas time was totally depressing. I had had the valves reground just a few months before, so I knew what I was in for, cost-wise.

These meetings I was to conduct for Raymond Fish, pastor of the St. Louis Church of God, represented the last dates I would have until the first of the year. Laura and I had calculated that we could have a nice Christmas for the girls if we were careful with our money. I had left her with about $30.00 to last the week I was away, and I had about the same amount in my pocket. I would stay with the pastor all week and eat at the parsonage, so I hadn't counted on any big expenses. Though I had agreed to come and conduct the meetings on faith and had no way of knowing how much I'd receive for my work, I was praying it would be at least $150.00. Now, with the prospect of paying $200.00 for car repairs, all those plans about the kids' Christmas gifts would have to be scrapped.

"Why now?" I asked God. Then, after a moment's reflection, I thought, "Why not? You've always taken care of our needs, and I know You will this time. I don't ask for special consideration for myself, Lord, but I sure don't want to disappoint the girls at Christmas. I know You'll help me somehow."

With that prayer, I felt better. I decided to "leave my burden" with Him, and when I pulled up in front of the church, I was ready to concentrate on the work at hand. I had come to St. Louis from Anderson on Sunday to dedicate the congregation's new church. Following the dedication, I was to conduct the services—doing both the preaching and the music from Sunday night through Friday night. It was the first time I'd ever tried to do both, having always worked with an evangelist before. I felt the pressure, but I was confident that I could handle it. A year ago, of course, I wouldn't have wanted any part of the preaching. Since my personal experience with Christ on the road to Middletown, I was bubbling over with good news, and I wanted to tell everyone about the Lord.

After the dedication service Sunday afternoon, I took the car to a Volkswagen dealer in Saginaw. The shop was open around the clock, so I told them I would be back to pick it up on Friday night. I knew I would not be able to pay the bill until after the meeting. In fact, I might be lucky to cover the cost with my honorarium for the week's services. I told the Lord He would just have to work it out.

Sunday night, I opened the service by telling simply and honestly what had happened in my life. The response reminded me of the services at East Side Church of God in

Anderson shortly after Laura and I began our reconciliation. The altar was lined with people who identified with the hypo-critical life I had been describing. It was the same all week. The meetings were not so big in terms of numbers, but the crowds grew a little each night. Many found their way to the Lord, and we were all rejoicing when we concluded the final service on Friday night. I was paid $150.00 which would have been just what we needed to buy groceries and the kids' Christmas presents, if I had not had the car repair bill ahead.

After the service, Fred Leppien and his wife, who had played the organ, volunteered to drive me to Saginaw to pick up the car. I was tempted to tell them my plight, but something restrained me. However, as we neared Saginaw, my worries increased. The mechanic had said, "Probably $185.00–$200.00, depending on the damage." Now, I began to wonder what I would do if he had underestimated the figure and I owed him more than that.

When we reached the garage, the service manager started up the engine. It sounded great.

"Okay," I said as we walked back to the office, "how much do I owe you?"

"I'll get the bill."

A moment later, he came back, smiling. "You're all set. That man over there took care of it." He motioned toward Fred. My heart came up in my throat, and I was hardly able to manage my expression of appreciation.

"Don't thank me," said Fred. "Thank the Lord, and when you have a chance, pass it on. Others have been mighty good to me over the years, and I'm just passing on some of their kindness. You'll have a lot of opportunities to do the same. Pass it on."

Then, as if they had not done enough already, when it came time to say goodbye, we shook hands and I felt a small piece of paper pressed into my hand.

"What's this?" I asked.

"Just a little something for your wife and kids' Christmas," Fred smiled. Once again, my eyes filled and words were inadequate. I climbed into the little, black Volkswagen and headed south with a song in my heart. A little farther down the road, I pulled over, turned on the light and looked at the check. I suppose I had expected about $20.00, and that would have been more than generous. The check read: $100.00.

We've had some wonderful Christmases in our family, but none so glorious as the Christmas of 1962. We had so much for which to be grateful. Little did I know that it was only God's beginning. I can't explain His goodness. I only know that you can't outgive Him. Once you commit your life to Him, His blessings flood in from every direction. I've come to call these unexpected gifts "God's extras" and often talk about them during meetings.

A few months later, I was in North Carolina for a series of meetings that would keep me away from home for four weeks. I was in Hickory with Omar Blevins. Following the Friday evening service, a woman asked me to sing at her church. The service was to be the next morning in the Seventh Day Adventist Church. It would have been an easy request to grant, but I didn't really want to make the effort.

"No, I'm sorry. I don't think I can make it," I lied.

Later in the evening, my conscience began to bother me and it seemed almost as if the Lord was rebuking me, "Did you turn her down because she was a Seventh Day Adventist?" In my heart, I had to confess my prejudice and I hurried to the phone to tell the lady I had reconsidered.

The next morning I received a tremendous blessing as I sang to her people. In spite of my selfishness in the beginning, I was again the recipient of one of "God's extras." The woman who had invited me to her church owned a fur shop. For coming to sing, she gave me a beautiful fur hat for Laura.

The next week at Drexel, North Carolina, there was more. On Sunday morning, I received a call from Anderson. Laura reported that she and the kids were huddled around the gas range because the furnace had gone out. I was already as homesick as I could be. The thought of my family shivering at home made me wish for them. When I mentioned the problem to one of the choir members, she said little but had soon put in motion an elaborate surprise. Unknown to me, a collection was taken, and Laura and the kids were flown in to spend the weekend with me. To welcome her, some of the girls had arranged a shower where she received more than ninety gifts!

While I was in North Carolina, I told a congregation about a frightening experience I had had a few weeks earlier on the Ohio Turnpike. Even though the Volkswagen was loaded with records and sound equipment (Fred Leppien had financed over $1000.00 worth of speakers, amplifiers and mikes), the car was too light to cope with the wind and rain of that night. Three different times, the storm caught the car and tossed it off the road onto the shoulder before I could stop it.

One person in the audience to hear this story was Guy Whitner, a lumber dealer from Newberry, South Carolina. Two weeks later, he handed me the keys to my first air-conditioned car, a new Chevrolet station wagon.

These examples of God's extras may indicate that I'm talking about material blessings only. The Lord has supplied all our needs in all areas, and sometimes in most spectacular ways.

I'll never forget some meetings Dad and I conducted in Portageville, Missouri. After the final service, he always wanted to go to a motel, get a good night's rest and then drive home or on to our next stop. I was always ready to keep moving. However, at Portageville, I deferred to his wishes, and we slept before driving on. About 3:00 A.M., Dad awoke, and not being able to go back to sleep, asked me if I wanted to get an early start. We packed hurriedly. Pulling out of the motel parking lot, I noticed that we had only a quarter of a tank of gas.

There were a couple of off-brand stations, but Dad suggested that we fill up at the junction of the interstate highway about thirty-five miles away.

When we reached the junction, there was no station open. We continued on, praying that we could find a gas station before the tank ran dry. But, by now, the needle was riding on empty.

"Lord, please give us a station over the next hill," I prayed aloud as the gas pedal stuttered.

"That's a wishful prayer," Dad teased. "There either is one or there isn't."

We didn't make it to the top of the hill, and the car coasted to a stop. It was a starless night, and the traffic on this road was very light. We might be there till morning, I thought. No sooner had we stopped than Dad was out of the car and running back down the road, waving at a pair of approaching headlights. The driver, a farmer, pulled his pickup truck to a stop. By the time I got out of the car, he and Dad were walking toward me with a five-gallon can of gas.

"It's about forty miles at least to the next gas station," he said. "I always carry a can of gas in the truck. Glad I came along when I did."

Not five minutes after we had run out of fuel, we were on our way. I poked Dad in the ribs with my elbow. "Well, God didn't build a gas station over that next hill. He chased us down the interstate with one!"

For nearly six years before Dad retired, I worked with him in many meetings. It was always refreshing for me because he was consistently good. Dad's perfectionist attitude left nothing to chance. He was earnest and diligent wherever he went in the service of the Lord. I was blessed with other fine associations in those days—such people as Billy Ball, Paul Jenkins, Dave Grubbs, Dan Harmon, Bill Jackson, Ernie Gross and Maurice Berquist. The crowds were not always large on the first night, but God blessed our efforts and people found the

Lord. Usually, the crowds grew as the meeting went along, and by the last Sunday, the church was packed.

There were some mighty small crowds, too. Once I was called to Plymouth, Indiana, for a Sunday night concert at the Baptist Church there. For some reason, I wasn't really looking forward to going. I had tried to beg off, but finally there were no excuses left. To make matters worse, it was snowing and sleeting on the way, and driving became extremely hazardous.

We slid into town about 6:30 P.M. Laura and Bill Gaither, who was playing piano for me, were along. We drove over to the church and sat there until 7:30, the starting time. Not one person came to the front door of the church.

"Maybe they have called the concert off," volunteered Laura.

It seemed logical, in view of the weather, so we drove downtown for dinner. As we were ready to leave the restaurant, I glanced at the restaurant clock. It read, 6:30.

"What time are you on here?" I asked.

"Daylight saving," the cashier replied.

We scrambled back into the car and drove back to the church. Lights greeted us from inside the church, and a few people were straggling in. The concert was received warmly. It was a touching evening. People tell me I do my best when the crowd is small. I hope so, because I believe it is important to do your best regardless of numbers. I do recall laughing at some of the statistics of that meeting. Of the thirty-nine people who attended the concert, twenty-nine bought albums. There was a "God's extra" from that experience, too. I had not expected to clear any profit at all after paying my pianist and other expenses. From past experience, a congregation of that size could not produce more than $10.00. To my amazement, someone in the group contributed a $200.00 check to our work, and my total honorarium was $211.00. It couldn't have come at a better time. We were down to our last few dollars, and God used Don and Noble Neidig to help us at a time when it was most needed.

Mentioning my good friend, Bill Gaither, reminds me of some memories we share about those days when we were both new to serving God through our musical talent. We both know what it is to perform before less-than-packed audiences.

For awhile, I traveled with the Bill Gaither Trio, giving concerts and special meetings across the country. It was great fun sharing the platform with Bill and Gloria and Dan, singing about God's love. Our witness may have been a little awkward, but it was sincere, and that's what counts. God blessed sincerity.

How well we recall the Bristow, Oklahomas and the Horse Creek, Tennessees! At Bristow, where we were expecting several hundred people, we had brought along enough sheet music and recordings to cover two long tables, anticipating the demand. Forty-eight people showed up! At Horse Creek, the crowd jammed—the first two rows! Nineteen people! To make that memorable evening complete, the record stand at the front door fell down, damaging some of our albums.

Bill and I had a little saying that we exchanged when the crowds weren't large. "Remember, play to the King." It refers to an often-told story about an English actor who refused to allow an understudy to take his part during a play in London, despite the small attendance.

"Take the night off," the director suggested. "The crowd is so small."

"No," replied the actor. "Those who have come deserve to see the cast which has been advertised."

The actor performed magnificently. The next day, a letter bearing a royal seal arrived at the theater. It was signed by the king. His Majesty had been an appreciative member of that small audience and had written to express his appreciation for a job well done. When you're working for the Lord, the King is always in the audience!

Bill Gaither and his music have figured prominently in my story. He, too, has been one of "God's extras." Without his friendship, his counsel, the inspired music he has written, his great lyrics I've been privileged to sing . . . well, it wouldn't have happened without Bill.

. I'll never forget the time Dad and I were conducting meetings in Marion, Indiana. Bill was teaching school in Alexandria during the day, driving to Marion in the afternoon to play for the meeting, and then returning home after the service. Bill had already shown considerable talent as a song writer. My father suggested a phrase that Bill might develop into a song. "See what you can do with 'He Touched Me.'" A few nights later, Bill appeared in Marion with a piece of music rolled under his arm. I hummed along as he played and then sang:

> *He touched me, oh, He touched me,*
> *And oh, the joy that floods my soul,*
> *Something happened, now I know*
> *He touched me and made me whole.*

The first time I heard that song, "it touched me." I sang it that night and, a few weeks later, recorded it. I didn't dream at the time how good that song was going to be to me and my family. "He Touched Me" was destined to become one of America's best loved gospel songs, and I was fortunate to be the first to sing it. Soon, it was requested everywhere I went.

In some ways, "He Touched Me" was responsible for bringing about my contract with the John T. Benson Publishing Company in Nashville, Tennessee. In 1967, they asked me to join them, and I cut my first album for them, including the song "He Touched Me." Without their help and the professional help of such people as Bob MacKenzie, my artist, repertoire man and producer, many of the good things that have happened since would not have resulted.

My first albums were recorded in Nashville, including "Something Worth Living For," which was to receive an award as the best gospel album of 1967. The sessions were later moved to London using the Philharmonic for background. Rick Powell and Ronn Huff have been my arrangers and conductors during these past years.

Bob Harrington, the chaplain from Bourbon Street, heard one of those early albums and liked it so well that he bought fifty albums to give to his friends. One of those friends was Jerry Falwell of Thomas Road Baptist Church in Lynchburg, Virginia.

Jerry was in Nashville on a day in 1970. While I was in a studio preparing for a session, he came by to invite me to Lynchburg.

"We'd like you to sing for us some Sunday morning. Give me a date. What's your first open Sunday?"

I tried to put him off, but, finally, in November of 1970, I agreed to sing. Jerry sent the church plane to Lima, Ohio where I had a Saturday night concert. After the concert, I flew to Lynchburg and sang in the Sunday morning service. At that time, the service was carried over a small network of seven Virginia TV stations.

Jerry asked me to come back in February for a three-day conference which he was holding and I agreed. In February, he asked me to sing regularly on the Sunday morning program, but I had a number of commitments which kept me from joining him at the time.

"Give me every Sunday you have open through the summer," he asked.

I found six open dates in June and July. Then, in September, he asked me once again to sing regularly on the program. The church plane would fly me to Lynchburg from wherever I happened to be singing on Saturday night. The Sunday service is aired as the Old-Time Gospel Hour. Jerry convinced me when he shared his elaborate plan—he envisioned the program being broadcast over hundreds of stations. His dream has been fulfilled and is being fulfilled as time goes on.

In September of 1971, when I began singing full-time on the Old-Time Gospel Hour, the program was viewed over thirteen television stations. Soon, the number had grown to fifty. Then, to more than one hundred. Two hundred. Three hundred. Today, the figure is four hundred-plus stations each Sunday. The program is beamed into millions of homes. This exposure has given me more opportunities to testify to the good news of Christ's saving power that I had ever imagined possible. When I think of the places God has led me since I surrendered to Him, I find it hard to believe. And to think—I questioned His ability to care for our family if I became a song evangelist. I have found that serving Him does not consist of the puny little things we do for Him, but in being constantly surprised at the amazing things he dreams for us.

It is going on eleven years since I brought Laura and the kids back home to Indiana to begin a new life. When we celebrate our wedding anniversary this fall—God willing—it will make our marriage about an even split—half hell and half heaven. Of course, the story of guilt and unrest being transformed to peace and usefulness is the story of anyone who comes to Him. The Bible tells about a few of them. Just the other day, I was reading from the 32nd chapter of Psalms. This passage has taken on new meaning, especially my friend Ken Taylor's translation of David's words in *The Living Bible.*

> What happiness for those whose guilt has been forgiven! What joys when sins are covered over! What relief for those who have confessed their sins and God has cleared their record.

> There was a time when I wouldn't admit what a sinner I was. But my dishonesty made me miserable and filled my days with frustration.

All day and all night your hand was heavy on me. My strength evaporated like water on a sunny day until I finally admitted all my sins to you and stopped trying to hide them. I said to myself, "I will confess them to the Lord." And You forgave me! All my guilt is gone.

Now I say that each believer should confess his sins to God when he is aware of them, while there is time to be forgiven. Judgment will not touch him if he does.

You are my hiding place from every storm of life; you even keep me from getting into trouble! You surround me with songs of victory. I will instruct you (says the Lord) and guide you along the best pathway for your life; I will advise you and watch your progress. Don't be like a senseless horse or mule that has to have a bit in its mouth to keep it in line!

Many sorrows come to the wicked, but abiding love surrounds those who trust in the Lord. So rejoice in him, all those who are his, and shout for joy, all those who try to obey him.

Not long after we picked up the pieces and began trying to reassemble them, we decided to move to Alexandria, a friendly town of six thousand, twelve miles north of Anderson. Bill and Gloria Gaither lived there with their children, and we decided it would be a wonderful place to bring up our own children. We bought a great, old house three or four blocks from the center of town. It was built around the turn of the century and had all the things old houses are supposed to have—big rooms, high ceilings, winding stairways and, most of all—character. We loved everything about it, starting with the swing on the front porch. Who needs air conditioning when you can swing on your porch and watch the world go by!

After we had moved just about everything to the new place, we went back to the old house in Anderson for the last time for a final check. It was an emotional time for us all; we were cutting ties with the past in more than one way. It was in this house that I had discovered my family had left me. It was in this room that I had found Laura's note. It was in this room I had threatened to take my life. There were some nightmarish moments that we were only too happy to leave behind. But it was also the place where our house had finally become a home.

As we walked around for the last time, we suddenly missed Dee Dee, our six-year-old.

"Where's Dee?" asked Laura.

"I don't know. I'll look for her," I answered.

In the living room, I found her hiding behind the front door, her little hands cupping the knob and her forehead pressed tightly against it. Her eyes were closed, and she was grimacing.

"What's the matter, Dee?"

"I don't like this place," she whimpered. "It scares me."

I knelt down and took her in my arms, drawing her close to me.

"Honey," I said, "it's not the house. It's the things that went on here that frighten you. You've got a new daddy now, and those things are all gone forever. I promise you. And you've got a new house. We don't live here anymore."

A few weeks later, I shared that experience with Bill Gaither. He said he'd like to recapture it in song and, some time later, handed me a piece of music. The title was "Thanks to Calvary, I Don't Live Here Anymore."

"Here's your song, Doug," Bill said. "Sing it."

I've been singing it ever since.

Today I went back to the place where I used to go,
Today I saw the same old crowd I knew before.

When they asked me what had happened, I tried to
*   tell them*
Thanks to Calvary, I don't come here anymore.
And then we went back to the house where we used to
*   live;*
My little girl ran and hid behind the door.
I said, "Honey, never fear, you've got a new Daddy.
Thanks to Calvary, we don't live here anymore."
Thanks to Calvary, I am not the man I used to be.
Thanks to Calvary, things are different than before.
While the tears ran down my face, I tried to tell her
Thanks to Calvary, we don't live here anymore.

(1.) Dale, Polly and Doug at the organ of the Dayton Church. (2.) A more recent family portrait. (3.) Taken the last Sunday before leaving Dayton to go to the Park Place Church of God, Anderson, Indiana. (4.) A flashy dresser at an early age.

4

3

(1.) The cottage at the campgrounds where Doug spent the summers. (2.) Doug and Laura Lee at her home in Nebraska the summer before they were married. (3.) Wedding bells.

1

2

(1.) Doug doing the morning show in High Point. (2.) Paula was only two weeks old when this was taken in North Carolina. (3.) Paula in a bucket at Huntington.

1.) Doug and his choir at the Glendale Church of God in Indianpolis, ready for the Christmas concert. (2.) Karen, Laura, Dee Dee, Doug and Paula at Christmas time while they were at the Glendale Church.

Opposite:
Some of the places Doug and Laura have called home; (1.) in Detroit, Michigan (2.) in Ashland, Kentucky (3.) and on the road.

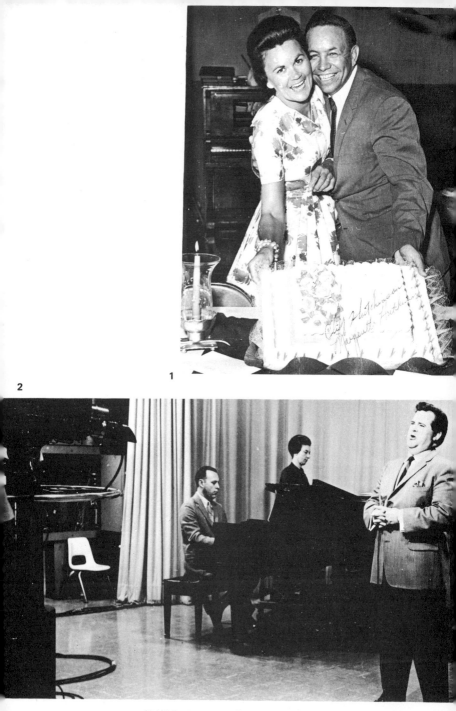

2

1

(1.) Margarette and Clifford Hutchinson, the pastor and his w
at Middletown, Ohio, who stood by Doug when Laura and
family had moved to Denver. (2.) Doug on TV on the Cad
Tabernacle program.

Doug singing on a missionary tour to Barbados, West Indies.
Doug and Laura at a reception with the McGuire Sisters.

*(1.) The Christian Brotherhood Hour Quartet as th[e]
appeared with the Pennsylvanians. (2.) Doug at t[...]
time.*

(1.) Fred Waring picture and autograph. (2.) The program book from the tour in 1955.

*(1.) Doug sings with his Dad.
(2.) Posters from two of the
many crusades and conferences
where they have teamed up.*

2

GOSPEL CONCERT

SATURDAY, JANUARY 27, 1968 -- 8:00 P.M.

Johns Hill Jr. High School

440 South Maffit Street at Johns Avenue, Decatur, Illinois

Presenting In Person

**Special Guest
Dr. Dale Oldham**
Speaker and Director of
Christian Brotherhood
Hour

Sunday -- 8:30 A.M.
WSOY

GAITHER TRIO
Alexandria, Indiana

DOUG OLDHAM
Anderson, Indiana

HENRY & HAZEL SLAUGHTER
Nashville, Tennessee

THE SONGMASTERS QUARTET
Decatur, Illinois

All Mail Orders:
Send Check or Money Order and
Self-Addressed, Stamped Envelope To:
PAUL G. PARR
P. O. BOX 855, DECATUR, ILLINOIS 62525

ALL RESERVED SEAT ADVANCE TICKETS . $1.50
RESERVED TICKETS AT DOOR $2.00
CHILDREN UNDER 12 YEARS $1.00

3

OLDHAM
CRUSA

A City-Wide Evangelistic Camp

Junior High School Auditorium
STILLWATER, OKLA.

Sunday, April 12, through Friday, April 17, 1
7:30 P.M. Each Evening

Dr. W. Dale Oldham

Doug

EVERYONE IS INVITED!

"WE WILL WORK W

(Sponsored by the CENTRAL DISTRICT CHURCHES OF

(1.) Doug and the Gaithers — Danny, Gloria and Bill — in concert. (2.) Paula Oldham and friend.

(1.) *Doug introduces his family at Thomas Road Baptist Church for the first time. (2.) Doug and Jerry Falwell, pastor of Thomas Road. (3.) Ministering to the congregation in Lynchburg.*

Televising the morning service at Thomas Road. (2.) Jerry Falwell and
, Jr. with Doug and Laura Lee in Mersin, Turkey in 1972 on a
ch-sponsored tour of the Holy Land.

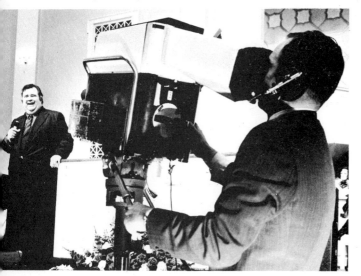

(1.) All the family in their house at Alexandria, Indiana. (2.) The old house that is the Oldham's house in Lynchburg, Virginia.